# Dark And Light

## Penny Golini

Copyright © 2024 by PENNY GOLINI

All rights reserved.

No portion of this book may be reproduced in any form without written permission from the publisher or author, except as permitted by U.S. copyright law.

# Contents

1. Younger — 1
2. Worrying — 12
3. The cure — 21
4. Something Strange — 32
5. The Beginning of the End — 46
6. The Beginning of The End Part 2 — 61
7. Powers? — 67
8. The End Fall — 78
9. Captured — 102
10. My Joy — 119
11. F*ck This Lab — 130
12. Escaped — 138
13. A year — 152

14. Not Any Longer . . . . . . . . . . . . . . . . . . . . . . . . . . . . . . . . . . . . . . . . . 166

# Younger

"Megan I don't care." I tell her as she continues eating her lunch.

"You're lying! You know you don't want him!" Megan said rather loudly.

I roll my eyes while giving her a knowingly look. I look back down at the cold, bland cafeteria food as I hear her ranting about how Logan don't love me and he ain't shit. She claims she is just looking out for me and that Logan would never love me the way I love him, but I beg to differ. She knows I don't plan on leaving him and she knows I don't care about what she thinks of him either.

"What about Liberty? You were so obsessed with her and wanted to be with her for the longest, and then Logan comes around and you don't like her anymore." She says trying to prove a point that won't get across.

"Megan we go through this every day, and every day it's still the same, I'm not leaving him," I say trying to get her to drop the subject, but sometimes I can't help but feel as if she has a point.

I did want Liberty, but the liking I took on her lead me nowhere. I remember thinking about the girl I did have a crush on for so long, just for her to not even give me enough attention. Megan used to encourage me to always talk to her but I could never bring myself to, I was just too shy. And yeah, there would be times in class were Liberty would ask if I need a piece of paper or me asking if she needed to borrow a pencil, but it never was more than that. She was my secret crush from freshman to Junior year, but she no longer holds importance to me as now all I think of was Logan.

I first saw him working during the latest summer while I was at the Waterpark. When I first looked into his eyes I couldn't look away no matter how hard I tried. He had this sort of pull that attracted you and could grasp you tight and never let go and I was curious to learn more. Soon later we hit it off and now the thought of Liberty was long gone and the constant rambling about Logan from Megan began.

"Oh now you got yourself a boyfriend and you don't want Liberty and I'm supposed to believe that." she says putting emphasis on the word boyfriend.

It doesn't even make sense to me anyways. Me and Logan have been together for about 4 months and yet she can't seem to stop talking bad things about him. She's barely even had a conversation with him and she still complains!

I groan and put my hands on my temple as I block out Megan. I stop stressing and turn my attention to the cafeteria and noticed how dull it looked. I mean it's highschool and no one is really the brightest at all times, but today everyone looked sick. I mindlessly motion for Megan but she's still talking.

"Megan shut up and look." I say leaning towards her and pointing to everyone ignoring her mean mugging me. "is it just me or does everyone look sick as a dog." I say noticing a lot of people sneezing occasionally and scratching their arms, sometimes their legs."Yeah

I think the flu going around or some like that" she says mindlessly observing the crowd.

I was gonna go deeper into it but decided to let it go. Maybe I was just getting worked up for no reason so I stop worrying and start a random conversation with Megan and I'm glad it doesn't include Logan. And just as I was thinking of him, I see Logan come up to our table from the corner of my eye.

"Hey Logan." I say with a bright smile to him as he's nearing closer to the table.

"Hey." he replies shortly as if he has something more important to say. He looks concerned, so I was going to ask him what's wrong before he cuts me off.

"Are you ok? Are you sick? Is there anything wrong with you?" He says nearly slapping my face to try to feel for some sort of symptoms.

"Wait- just wai- boy get your hands away from me." I blurt out trying to stop the attack on my face

"I'm sorry it's just I overheard the front office talking about something serious that could affect us all." Megan and I both look at him signaling him to continue. "They said some type of virus is spreading all over the globe that broke out just about 3 weeks ago and is infecting too many people in such little time." He claims still looking worriedly over my face.

I start to think back to a few days when I was watching the news with my dad. The news reporter said some new virus we don't know about was spreading but wasn't too big of a risk, but I didn't think much of it because it didn't seem like much until now.

"Are you for real?" Megan says in complete shock. Logan then turns his direction towards her now realizing she was right next to me. "If you don't mind me asking, is this virus deadly." She says trying to grasp what he was saying to her.

I know for a fact Megan is about to panic. She has had an issue with taking shocking news lightly ever since a robber came and shot both her parents while at school. It was freshman year and we were walking home at the time and saw the police cars and they told us what had happened. And to add on her older sister, Brooklyn, who was at college when this happened had to become the legal guardian of Megan and their younger sister Kalaya. Brooklyn couldn't handle the responsibility of watching Megan and Kalaya, and then deal with the death of her parents so she ended her life.

To say it was a very hard year for Megan was an understatement. She and her sister had to go into foster care. When we made it to senior year she still wasn't 18, yet the court allowed her to get emancipated from foster care, but wasn't able to get her sister out until she is 18 which isn't too far away. She obviously went into therapy and got some help, but in situations with death knocking at the door she panics too much and thinks irrationally.

"No! What are we going to do!? How-" I stop her before she can go on and psych herself out. I turn towards my best friend who is violently shaking. I gently wrap my arm around her shoulders and rub her arms slowly.

"Megan I think we'll be alright, we just gotta be safe okay." I say to her reassuringly and gently pat her shoulders before slowly letting go. She looks a little more calmed down and stares at the floor blankly. I then look back up at Logan and try to make sense of the news I heard.

Logan looks at me sympathetically before speaking up about the issue again. "I actually really think we might need to quarantine and stay away for a bit this virus is rapid and deadly." Megan then looks at Logan with wide eyes before going back to aggressively shaking. I look back up at Logan in disbelief. He totally meant to do that.

"Why would you do that? I just got her to calm down!" I say scolding him and he looks at me obviously not caring about what he said. I put my arms around her again repeating what I did before to calm her down, but this time she lowly talks to herself saying random words.

Logan has a small smirk pulling at his lips not showing it all the way. I then hear the speakers in the cafeteria go off. "Students this is principal Brettman and I'm here to give you some devastating news. As some of you might've heard, a virus that is going around is deadly and is moving rapidly. If you have symptoms of sneezing, bipolar temperature, and a red rash along your legs and arms instantly stop what you are doing and come to the office now without touching anything. Everyone else stay at a distance and get home safely, please and thank you" I hear the coms go off and the whispers of students start. I see a bunch of people getting up either to go to the office or home.-

As we pass the trees and houses of my neighborhood. I look down at me and Logan's hand. I mesmerize by the way his hand feels on mine. I let go of his hand putting my hand on his cheek while staring at him. I love the way his skin feels on mine. He stops walking and looks at me worriedly.

"Are you sure you're going to be okay Joy?" He asks holding my hand close to his cheek. I nodded my head not trusting my voice due to the panic I was feeling. He then, with his other hand started to brush my face putting a braid behind my ear and kiss my forehead. Thank God he can't see me blush right now. I give him a small smile before we continue walking. As we continue our track to home I pull out my phone to distract myself from the events today when I see 3 missed calls from my dad. I'm really hoping that my father is just checking up on me and nothing more. I now stop walking and call him instantly.

"Hey Joy sweetheart, are you ok do you have any symptoms?!" He questions frantically. My father is a nurse and works constantly to help other people. I believe he wanted to help more and more ever since my mother died and I appreciate the efforts he makes for me and my sisters."Yeah I'm all good are you and the girls ok?" I reply."Yeah I'm just glad your ok im going be at the house in about 20 min I'll see you there." He hangs up the phone and I turn back to Logan

"Everything all right, do you want me to come home with you?" He asks.

"Nah I'm just going to go home by myself, I'll see you later." I say reaching up on my tiptoes and peck his small lips. He smirks down at me and pulls me closer before kissing me longer. I pull away and smile a bit before I let him go and trail to my house.-

About an hour later of me being home I hear the front door open. I walk downstairs and see my younger sisters, Mya and Octavia.

"Joy! We missed you!" Mya and Octavia yell.

"Hey guys how was school was it fun?" I say relieved to see them in perfectly good shape. I advert my attention behind them and see my father drained out. I look back at my sisters, "How about you guys go in the kitchen real fast while I talk to daddy, then you can tell me about your day." I say giving them a soft smile. They took off into the kitchen and before I can say something he speaks up first.

"Sorry it took so long there was a lot of traffic." My dad says tiredly.

"It's alright you guys are home now that's all that matters." I say with a smile on my face. Shifting my weight on my feet, "Dad so so you think we'll be alright? I mean with what's going on right now I don't really know what to think to be quite honest."

He looks down and me up pinches between his eyes. "I, um- I want to believe that we are ok but- Joy there is some stuff going on right now that us nurses and doctors cannot explain." I furrow my brows a bit trying to register my thought process into a sentence.

"Dad are we going to be alright?" I ask hoping for the best answer possible.

He pats his hand on my shoulder with tears threatening to spill out from his eyes. "We need to be with each other right now most, I don't know what is going to happen with this virus Joy, and I don't know how to explain this to anyone really, but I need you to put trust in me and this family, ok?" With my brows still furrowed I nod my head even though I am still confused.

My dad faces towards the kitchen wiping down the tears that managed to fall. "Ok who wants hamburgers for dinner" he yells from the living room while walking to the kitchen.

"I do!""Yeah me too!" my sisters yell happily.

I think about the words my father just said and can't help the feeling of despair bubbling in my stomach. I force myself to push it away and get started on helping my dad cook to keep some sort of normalcy before things go downhill.-

One thing I hate is being awoken from my sleep. My day obviously wasn't the best as I realized we could all possibly be dying and not to mention that weird little speech my dad gave me. So when I turn to see who the hell is calling me almost at 3 in the morning my tone isn't gonna be the nicest. I groggily turn on my back and snatch my phone from the charger. I didn't even check who it was before I pressed accept and start talking.

"Whoever you are, you best have a reason as to why you waking me up this late." I say half asleep. I then hear sniffling on the other end of the phone and wake up a bit more. I then realized that the crying belongs to my best friend.

"Megan, what going on, what's wrong!?"

"Joy I think I got this virus." she says while crying.

..

# Worrying

"Megan what do you mean you think you have this virus?" I say scared of my friends safety.

"I mean I woke up in the middle of the night hot and sweaty, then I turned really cold and started sneezing a lot! And then I started itching and have this red rash over my arms!" She said wavering her voice a bit.

I blink not being able to register what I just heard. I didn't want to believe what was happening to her.

"Joy, are you there?" She said quietly.

"Yea, yes I'm still here i- I just dont know what to say right now." I say on a verge of tears.

"Look I hope I am just being over dramatic. Maybe I was just having a cold or something, imma get a good nights rest and if I don't feel better I won't go to school and I'll be at the doctors, ok Joy so no need to get worried."

"Ok, just be safe alright" I sigh shaking my head.

"Ok, goodnight Joy"

"Goodnight Megan."

I put my phone down and the next thing you know I feel tears forming until they are falling from my ears freely. What if Megan actually leaves me? I never thought about since I've always thought she'll be by my side forever. She was one of the only girls who stood up for me. We've been friends for so long I dont want her to leave me. I don't know what I would do.

I couldn't go back to sleep even if I wanted to so I pick up my phone again and call Logan hoping he would pick up. I hear him pick up the phone with a tired voice "Why are you calling me, it's about to be 4 in the morning love. "

"I um- I need to be with you right now." I say choking on my own words.

I hear rustling on the other side of the phone like hes getting up."Wait what happened, are you ok?!" He says in a worried voice.

"Yeah I'll be fine after I see you. can I please come over." I beg desperately.

"Yeah of course you can come over just be quiet because my brother and sister are sleeping"I start smiling feeling a little better.

"Yeah I'll be quiet I got you. Bye logan I love you."

"I love you too."

I get up and get dressed like I am going to school and then brush my teeth as quietly as I can. After I'm all done I grab my phone, a charger and some headphones, with my backpack and leave. I slowly walk downstairs without trying to wake anyone and I climb out of a window downstairs that doesn't make any noise when I open it. I get out and start walking to Logan's house. He doesn't live very far from me so I'm able to see him plenty.

Soon I see his house and call him telling him that I'm outside.

"Hey you outside yet?" He says

"Yeah where do I go in?" He then tells my to go to the side of the house where his bedroom is. I walk my way over there and see that he has the window open for me. I climb into the room and shut the window behind me.

When I turn around I see logan standing right behind me with his bare chest smiling right at me. I stumble back a little bit taken by surprised. He clearly sees what effect he has on me and starts chuckling lowly while putting his hands around my waist pulling me closer. He puts his head in the side of my neck and inhales deeply. As long as I knew logan he always does this. It's like a comfort thing for him to know that I'm near him.

"Hey" I said nervously

"Hey" he said in a deep tired voice. In all honesty I could listen to him talk like that all day long.

"Why were you crying earlier." he said just now remembering

"Um Megan called me and said that she thinks she has this virus and if shes not feeling well tomorrow then she wont come to school." I say about to cry again.

His eyes widen when he sees the tears falling down. He puts his thumb underneath my eyes and wipes the tears falling from them. He pulls me back into a bone crushing hug and rubs my back slowly.

"I'm pretty sure she is going to be okay Joy, she is pretty strong you know. Remember when she had to take a final but had a fever and even though the school said she could retake it later she denied and she straight up took the test while burning up and coughing." He says trying to lighten up the mood.

I chuckle thinking of that day. She'll be damned if she had to come in on her summer break to take a final later.

"Come on let's lay down for a bit." He says letting go of me and we go sit on his bed. I take off my shoes and lay back on the bed with him.

"So what about rereading our favorite book again?" Logan asks with his eyebrows raised and a smirk.

I nod my head while chuckling a bit "Yeah, I haven't read in a while."

He pulls me by the waist and I lay my head on his chest while he starts reading a corny child book that we both apparently used to love when we were younger. Sometimes I wish it can always be like this, relaxed. Its calm and no one can mess this moment up because it's me and him, forever......"Lily the fuck you mean he got a girl in his bedroom?!" I woke up and saw the book that Logan was reading on his chest and a loud voice yelling. I just realized we really fell asleep reading and we have been caught. I then understood what was just said and I try to hurry and stand up to go hide before his brother comes into the room. I seem to have woke up Logan with all of the movement going around in th bed.

"What are you doing Joy, what's going on?" He says tiredly

"Your brother Luke, that's what's going on! I guess your little sister saw me in the room when she was trying to wake you up or something and told your brother!" I say whisper yelling

"Shit hurry up and go into the bathroom" he says also whisper yelling.

"Imma beat his ass if I find a girl in his room!" Then I hear footsteps coming up real fast. I try to hurry and get out of bed and run into the restroom, but as I got out of the bed I trip on the sheets and land straight on my face.

"Fuck!" I yell rather loudly. I groan and try to stand up to relieve the pain on my face.

"Shit, Joy are you ok?" Logan says rushing over to pick me up and inspect my face.

"The fuck going on in here?" Luke says wanting an answer and not even considering trying to help my injured face.

"Who the fuck is she!?" Luke yells loudly. Coming in more to the room as he sees me crouched down on the floor with a half naked Logan next to me.

I try to get up, but Logan picks me up first and puts me on his bed with him turning to go look at his brother.

I see Lily come into the room and her eyes look straight at me.

"Oh hey Joy, I didnt know that it was you sleeping in here" she says laughing a bit "I thought Logan was cheating on you with another girl!" She says confusingly.

I stare blankly at the little girl. She should've thought about double checking who I was before she went and told, and now I'm stuck with a bruised face.

"Lily you know her?" Luke says confused. Lily looks up at her brother and nods her head proudly.

"That's Joy, Logans girlfriend isn't she pretty." Lily says smiling up at him.

I was supposed to meet Luke very soon for dinner since Logans parents are out of town and Luke is watching over them. Luke lives in a different state and I'm assuming her came here to visit and get to know what happening with Logan and the family before their parents went out of town.

"Sorry for yelling I didnt know you were my little brother's girlfriend." he says rubbing the back of his head.

I chuckle a bit and replied. "Yeah sorry, wish we could've meant under better circumstances." I say with a smile on my face.

"Yeah me too, um sorry about this again." he says standing awkwardly in the room.

Logan coughs to get our attention."Can you guys like leave now." he says directly to his siblings. Luke looks at him and nods.

"Before I leave can I ask you guys question?" Me and Logan look at each other and shrug our shoulders.

"Did you guys have sex on the bed." My eyes open widely and Logan turns red. Luke busts out laughing while turning away from us.

"I'm just kidding you guys should've seen yall faces." he says laughing a bit more.

"But seriously if you guys did I hoped you used condoms." he said while walking out of the door and closing it shut.

I look at Logan and he shakes his head in embarrassment.

"He seems sweet."......

# The cure

After our little incident at Logans house we left and went to go eat some Dunkin' donuts. On the way there I realized my dad doesn't know I left house early so I called and lied to him that I left early because I wanted to go on a walk before I went to school to clear my head from yesterday.

After I get off my phone I look to see Logan staring at me.

"Is everything all right?"

"Yeah he thinks I went to go on a walk."

"Wow you actually lied to him that surprising." Logan says grabbing me and pulling me in at the waist while kissing my forehead.

Logan knows that I don't like lying to my dad, but sometimes lying leads to less questions, and that's how I like it.

We make our way up the line and order our food. We walk back to school and I look up to see my bestfriend and she doesn't look to sick. I jump up and let go of Logans hand and run up to her.

"Hey" she say smiling brightly.

"Hey" I say smiling just as bright

"Your not sick anymore." I say scrunching my eyebrows in confusion.

"No I'm not anymore, guess why!" She says smirking.

"Why?" Logan asks coming to stand right besides me

"I wasn't asking you, I was asking Joy, Lucas." Megan says sharply staring daggers at him. Logan goes to say something but I cut him off so an argument doesn't start between the two.

"You know his name is Logan, Megan but why?

"Because the school is handing out the cure to students!" She says happily.

"Wait are you for real?" I say shocked.

"Yes bitch I'm for real. They got everybody in there, doesn't matter if your sick or not and when i took it I instantly felt relief."

I was going to get excited and join in on her happiness until I start to think a vital question. How the hell did they get a cure so damn fast? And are vaccines every supposed to work that fast?

"Wait how did they get a cure that fast? I say asking my question out loud.

Megan and Logan both look at me and start to look confused just like me.

"Yeah that is true huh? I'm just hoping they got it fast because the virus was moving rapidly and they didn't want people dying quickly. But you're right Joy, that is kinda weird." says Megan

"Well should we go and take it?" I say confused.

"I mean we have to it's the law the government made it mandatory."

I look at Logan and Megan unsure this all seems kind of shady, but if they are forcing us to taking it I don't know what we can do.

Logan looks down at my uncertain face and shakes his head in disapproval "No we are going home, you look uncomfortable. " He said taking me to the the car.

"Wait, they are going to give you the cure whether you like it or not, they have a roster and if you name isn't checked then they'll go to your house and make sure you take it." Megan said running after us.

"And how the hell do you know all of that. Logan says already unlocking his car.

"It's on the paper they give you-" She shut the door that Logan just opened and stares at him. Logan stares back with a 'what the fuck' look before Megan rolls her eyes and sighs deeply trying to reason with us again.

"Come on you guys just get it over with I took the cure and look, I got better, also the people from yesterday don't have any symptoms, and if something terrible does happen then it happens to all of us." Megan says trying to reassure us.

"And that will convince me to take this how?" Logan said obviously irritated with Megan. I walk up between them, grab Logan's hand to calm him down and face Megan.

"Its fine. It's not that big of a deal we'll go."......

We walk inside the school and the place that is supposed to be the cafeteria is filled with a bunch of students in seperate lines. Megan went in and decided to go to her classes since she already took the cure. Me and Logan walk hand in hand into a line with a fair amount of students.

I get closer to Logan and lean on his shoulder and he rubs my arm comfortably. We wait in line a little longer until we get to the front where there was a mid sized, brown hair, tan skinned lady in front who seems to be a doctor. She has a clipboard in her hand but doesn't look up to me or Logan.

I look confused at Logan and give him a suggestive look that we should go inside the room. When I step to enter the room the lady puts the clipboard out to stop me from moving and speaks with a smooth British accent. "What is your name please?" She said in a monotone voice.

"Logan Jackson and Joy Pierre." Logan speaks up for the both of us.

She looks up with her dark brown eyes, eyeing the two of us.

"Sorry the room is full right now and we need one more person not two more people, one of you is going to have to wait your turn." She said then looked back down at the clipboard obviously not caring that much.

"Well I'm sorry, but can we wait until there is two spots open. I want to take the cure with Joy." Logan spoke up in an agitated voice.

"I'm sorry, but I did just say only one of you guys can go in, so if one of you will just please get inside the room. Others are waiting to get the cure too." She said staring at us in a way that left no room for an argument, but of course Logan being Logan spoke back.

He looks at her again more irritated than the last time and raises his voice a bit. "I just asked if we can wait I don't see the big deal in that Mary Poppins." Logan said making fun of her accent.

That seemed to have sent her over the edge as she scrunches her eyebrows putting the clipboard down on a wooden stool near her legs.

" I don't know who the hell you kids think you are-"

"What is going on here?" A voice said loudly interrupting the doctor.

I turn around to see a tall, white male, with green eyes and a long beard looking at the 3 of us. The man was wearing a lab coat similar to what the previous doctor seemed to be wearing but he had a small black name tag that read 'William Whittaker'. I look back up to his eyes and sense a strange feeling. This man looked like he wouldn't show any emotion with the way his eyes traveled between the three of us like he was looking at prey.

The lady who tried to yell at us immediately went in front of us towards him and explained everything to him, stumbling over her words.

"Sorry Dr. Whittaker I was just trying to tell them that the ro- room is full and that only one- one person can enter, but that boy didn't want to li- listen I'm sorry." She said frantically with her head bowed down at the end.

He nods his head understandably rubbing his beard looking at me and Logan. "Hmm I see and who might these kids be?" He said eyeing us up and down. His eyes traveled rather creepily across me and I start to feel uncomfortable and hug my body looking at the ground. Dr. Whittaker took a step towards us and Logan noticed it and stepped in front of me. Dr. Whittaker came in front of him and stared at him for a while.

"Lindsey," he called out. And the lady from before quickly stepped over to us.

"Let these people in together, and take them to the back rooms." He said sternly.

I look up confused as to why he requested we go to the backroom, but I didn't have the heart to speak up about it unlike Logan who questioned it.

"Why the hell are we going to the back room?" He asked, more like demanded from him.

"Well you guys said you wanted to take it together. Just go with her before I change my mind boy." He said eyeing Logan once again.

If I was in Logan's situation I would feel rather intimidated by Dr. Whittaker due to the fact that he is tall and has a menacing look in his eye, but Logan obviously isn't. I don't know if it's the fact that Logan has muscles for days and can handle himself or he simply just doesn't feel threatened by him.

"I think you should be aware of how you talk to us." Logan says just as threatening.

Dr. Whittaker smirks with his dry thin lips "You gotta strong heart boy I'll give you that. Get these kids a the cure and don't make me have to tell you again understand Lindsey." he said dismissing Logan while looking towards Lindsey irritated.

Logan looks at him with a cold stare he looks like he isn't going to move and continue to argue with Dr. Whittaker. I don't really want to go into the backroom and would rather stay where everyone else is at, but I also don't want to start some type of argument with this doctor, he looks threatening.

I go to grab Logan's hand and pull him towards me. I walk in front of him and look directly at Dr. Whittaker's eyes.

"We are sorry for the inconvenience, and we will just go to the backroom and take the cure there." I say trying not to let my voice show my fear.

"You better listen to her boy she seems to have more common sense then your ass." He says still looking at me but talking to Logan. "Go with Lindsey there will be other people back there if you are feeling worried." I know the intention behind his words were supposed to sound calming and reassuring, but I can't help the shivers that run up my spine when he speaks.

Logan goes to step in front of me again but I push him back pleading for him to let this go with my eyes. Logan has a tad issue with people disrespecting me or making me feel uncomfortable. And by a tad bit I mean a lot. I get in these type of situations often where I find myself not wanting to say anything or feel reluctant to stand up for myself, but Logan will dismiss what I feel and end up standing up for me. And it's not like I can't stand up for myself or want to, it's just easier to let people get their way without a conflict happening, but everytime I think I avoided a conflict Logan comes right back up to start it again.

"Are you sure you're ok with this?" Logan asked me holding my hand to his chest.

"Yes Logan let's just get this over with." I say trying to convince him. He looks over my pleading eyes and nods his head slowly. He lets go of my hand that's on his chest and replaces it with his other hand by his side and pulls me towards where Lindsey is at. He looks at her signaling to go through the room. She nods in understanding and walks inside the room with us behind her trail. Before we walk fully into the room I hear Dr. Whittaker speak to us.

"I'll be seeing you guys soon." He says in a low deep voice. Logan and I both stop walking and he turns around to look at him, but when he goes to turn around there was no one there........

# Something Strange

Lindsey takes us into the room where all the students are getting their shots. As we are passing by them I see a weird blue-ish blackish shimmery liquid inside the needles. The color is a little weird to me, especially for a cure, but I'm not going to question too much on it.

We made our way through the room to another door inside the room that was in the back. Lindsey opens it up with a keypad that was on the side of the door typing in a bunch of numbers. When did our school get this?

She let's us inside and I see how very few students are in here, unlike the other room. I start to feel that uneasy feeling again and try to push it down. I was just nervous and had to breath, but the way I was feeling right now made breathing feel impossible.

I take a step into the small room that was littered with tiny scratches on the plain gray walls that had dust cloud the room. I tried to calm myself down by breathing deeply but the dust that filled the room took me by surprise and I instantly starting to cough.

"Joy are you alright?" Logan asks holding on to my arm so that I don't trip and fall over me coughing. I put my hand on my chest with my free hand and nod my head.

"I'm fine just a little dusty in here." I say pulling myself up I look up around the room again and see that everyone I staring at me weirdly. I then realize that they probably think I have this damn virus the way I was just coughing.

I start to feel my cheeks heat up and I clear my throat."Sorry guys I don't have the virus the rooms a little dusty, kinda making me cough. Don't yall think?"

I said stopping myself because now they were looking even more weirdly at me. Clearing my throat awkwardly, I look to the side of me and see Logan trying to keep in a smile that was threatening to come out anytime. I hit the side of his arm to stop him and he turns to look at me before giving me a big grin shrugging his shoulders. I roll my eyes at him and turn back towards Lindsey.

"Um, ok anyways, you guys are going to go over there with Olivia to take the vaccine." Lindsey said pointing to the left side of the room in the back corner where a small, young blond woman was standing. I couldn't get a good glimpse of what she looked like from over where I was standing, but she seemed very fidgety and timid.

"Yeah, okay I'm just gonna go over there now." I say sheepishly smiling. I clear my throat again before I grab Logan's hand going to the left side of the room where Olivia was at. As we are walking up to her I notice she seems to be more visibly fidgety as she goes backs and forth from biting her nails to her playing with her hair.

"Hi, take a seat here." Her voice also seemed almost nervous like she is planning on talking to a crowd of people. I choose to ignore it as she is pointing to the small chair next to a bunch of surgical items. I gulped looking at the tray next to the chair. I really hate going to the doctors and having them poke and prob me with their tools. I start to think back to when I was younger and my mother would force me to sit down just so the doctors could take my tempature. No need to say that I really can't stand the doctors, especially needles.

I go to take a seat just to get the shot over with first, but Logan comes from the side of me and sits in the chair first. I look at him and he looks back up at me smuggishly.

"I was going to sit there Logan."

"I know but you seemed nervous so I'm going to go before you." He said leaning back in the chair comfortably.

"Whatever." I mumble lowly secretively grateful he took the seat before I did. I turn towards Olivia seeing her grab the same blue-ish blackish shimmery liquid that I seen in the previous rooms. She grabs the needle and flicks it a bit ready to insert it into Logan.

"Ok stay seated, I'm going take some of your diagnostics real fast and then I will stick the needle in your arm. Also before we start, you need to come back tomorrow to take another one for the vaccine to work fully." When she is finished explaining, she does all the doctor check up things. She goes to type something in the computer when all of a sudden she gasps lowly. I look over to the computer screen to see why she's gasping but she quickly turns it off turning her attention to us.

"What is something wrong?" I ask still wondering.

"No- no of course nothings wrong. Im just going to put this needle in your arm, don't move." She ssys dismissing my question and working on Logan. She gets prep to put the needle in his arm before she stops and looks at him with glimpse of guilt flash between her eyes. "Please tell me if you feel anything strange I want you to be a 100 percent safe."

I furrow my eyebrows at that. I didn't like that sentence it was very strange. I wanted to tell her stop, but I looked at Logan who didn't seem to mind or notice what she had said to him. I suck in a breath as she gets close to him to stick the needle in. She puts the shot in and I turn my face up. I hate the way needles go through the skin, it makes me feel icky so I look away until I feel Logan grab my arm. He was finished and gave me a reassuring smile.

"All done. See nothing to be afraid of." He said rubbing my arm with his thumb.

"Did it hurt?" I ask for my own comfort.

"It's a shot Joy it doesn't hurt very bad. Just sit here and get it done. I will be here the whole time." He says standing up from the little chair.

Obviously I know how a shot feels, but I kinda get thrown off about the fact that something so tiny is going through my skin and making it tear. I just don't like it. I shake my head and go to sit in the chair Logan was previously sitting in.

She gets prepped just like she did with Logan's shot. Logan grabs my hand in his and looks down at me with a small smile. I smile back and turn my head away from the needle with my eyes closed.

I breathe in and wait for the small, sharp pain, but yet there wasn't any pain. It almost felt good. It felt like it was pulsing out jolts of joy through all of my veins and every inch of my body rapidly.

I look down at my arm and feel the sensations going through my body at the moment. I can feel it everywhere. It felt like if you were a kid playing on the playground and eating your favorite food. It made me feel almost happy, excited, exhilarated? I was so in my own world that when I finally look up, I see Logan falling to the ground besides me.

The small table next to us gets punched as all the items on it fall onto the ground next to him screaming in pain. He held his stomach as his crouched to the floor groaning. I immediately fall to the ground and sit by him patting his back looking in panic.

"Logan, Logan what's happening, what's wrong!" I say about to cry. I look up to find Olivia and notice she is now across the room making some type of medicine with a clear white liquid.

I was going to say something to her before I hear him scream louder this time, in more agonizing pain. The veins across his body were starting to glow, sparkling underneath his skin. I can see the blackish and blueish tint flowing through his face like a bug was crawling underneath it.

I jump off him, scooting away to take in what I just saw, and if what I just saw was my boyfriend glowing I don't think I can take it in. Everyone in the room instantly gets quiet and stares at Logan in confusion and in shock. I see that Olivia quickly comes back with a small, bottle filled, clear liquid. She lays next to the ground by Logan and forces him to drink it.

"Logan drink it, all of it." She says forcefully shoving it in his mouth. Logan drinks all of it and starts coughing.

"I'm alright." He says coughing a little bit. I get pulled out of my shock now that I see he is alright and slowly pull him up, hugging him tight. He holds me close and lays his head in my shoulder tiredly. I stay there and rub his back until I just realized what really had happened.

"What the hell happened to him" I say demanding answers from anyone who could possibly give me one.

"I'm sorry. I knew it. I knew this would happen from the tests we made and his diagnostics that this would have some serious effect. His veins were bubbling up and he shouldn't be standing, but he's alrigh-." She says cutting her mumbling short "He's alright, he is okay nothing bad happened!" Olivia says realizing something important. I stare back at her confused as to what the hell she was talking about, but then I heard small whispers from the room coming from the other doctors.

I wanted some type of answer and the doctors are rambling and whispering that Logan is fine like he shouldn't be. Why is him being alright so shocking? Olivia turns around smiling brightly at me then her face drops as she realizes what she just said.

I look at her confused again and she goes to say something until all of a sudden Dr. Whittaker steps inside the room with his long lab coat. He scans across the room until his eyes land on me and Logan laying on my shoulder. His eyes widen at the look of Logan and a small smirk plays at the side of his lips. He steps over to us and grabs Logan's shoulder turning Logan towards him inspecting his face. Logan still being drained from whatever just happened doesn't stop Dr. Whittaker from grabbing him as he is to out of it.

Because Logan doesnt know whats going on I reach out to grab him away from Dr. Whittaker , but he puts his hand up signaling me to stop."Not one side effect. Strange."

I look yet again confused as he grabs Logans jaw turning his face in different directions, getting a good look at him. I instantly get weirded out and grab Logan pulling him towards me again not caring what Dr. Whittaker says.

"I knew it would work, I could just tell he was the one." he says to more himself than us.

"Ok I don't know what is going on here, but I would like an explanation now." I say with crossed arms eyeing Dr. Whittaker demanding that he explains. Instead of answering me he turns to Olivia who listens intently as they are whispering something in secret. I start to get pissed that he is ignoring me, so I step next to him getting closer.

"I know you heard me. What happened!" I say no longer caring to ask in a nicer way.

"Nothing you need to worry about Ms. Pierre, just some exciting news to us doctors." He says promptly turning back around to Olivia.

This wasn't enough information for me so I grab his shoulder and make him turn towards me. I stare at him right in his eye showing that I am wanting actual answers. "That is not a good enough answer. Tell me a good reason for what I just saw because it wasn't normal." I say in the most demanding voice I can put on while trying not to show any sign of fear.

He obviously looks annoyed with me as he doesn't seem to find me threatening in the slightest. He sighs while rubbing his head with his palm. "Ms. Pierre if you would be as so kind to come here tomorrow with Logan and then I will explain this to you." He said in a monotone voice, not caring about what I think.

I look at him like he's crazy. We are not coming here again especially with how secretive they are acting. Logan was just on the floor, and his veins were literally glowing. If he thinks we are coming back he got another thing coming to him. Forget the second shot at this point. I refuse to put Logan or I in this situation again.

I scoff in belief and chuckle, shaking my head to myself. "We arent staying here any longer or coming back here tomorrow, forget whatever weird shit yall got going on in here." I say going back to Logan ready to leave this room. I put his arm around my shoulder getting ready to help him walk. He weakly holds on and still lays his head on my shoulder a bit.

"Tomorrow you are coming here, both of you." Dr. Whittaker said as I'm nearing closer to the door.

I turn my head back around staring at him pissed off. "What if we don't?" I say challenging him.

He looks me dead in the eye leaving me with shivers running down my back again. "You know if you don't come back tomorrow, he is going to have another one of those episodes again and second time around it ain't pretty. But if you want that to happen again and you don't want to know more, be my guest."

I look around the silent room I can't have what just happened happen to Logan again. I don't even know how to fix it if it does happen again. Olivia gave him a clear liquid that I do not know what it was made of. Us not coming tomorrow would be stupid if it meant putting Logan in danger, but Dr. Whittaker might just be lying so that we can come again tomorrow. I decide not to give him an answer and walk out the quiet room giving him one last glance.

We walk away from the lines and go inside in one of the staff's bathrooms to check on Logan. "Hey you ok, can you stand straight up?" I ask him removing his arm from my shoulder.

"Yeah yeah I'm think good." he says reassuring me. I slowly let go of him but rest my hand on his back.

"What do you think they did to you?" I say reaching up to his face to inspect it.

"I assume what they did to you, but you obviously didn't feel what I felt." He said breathlessly. He was right though. I didn't feel what he felt. I felt rather good actually on the contrast to him.

"What exactly did you feel Logan?" I say moving his hair out of his now sweaty face.

"It felt like pain seering through my whole entire body. The blood in my veins felt as if they were bubbling getting hotter and hotter by the second. It honestly felt like I was being burned on the inside out." He said with his face turns up reminiscing the pain. I copy his actions thinking about how much pain that must be and the way it felt.

"What did it feel like for you?"

I think back to my experience. Why did it feel so good for me, but absolute hell for him. It made me want to question, but the only person who has answers is a creepy, middle- aged, white man who is probably into some weird shit. I want to answer truthfully about what it felt like, but the way I felt was something I never felt before, it was euphoric. I kinda want to go tomorrow just to feel the way I felt again, but I am not tryna risk me turning into a crackhead. So because I also don't want to sound like I'm already addicted I give Logan a short answer.

"It felt fine, normal really." Logan nods his head looking at me with uncertainty. I look away from him knowing that he probably knows I'm lying. He always gives me a certain look when he thinks I am lying and somehow breaks it out of me every single time. I just hope this time I'm strong enough not to cave in.

"Alright Joy, let's get to class." He says grabbing my hand leading us out the restroom......

Ok soooo what so you think is happening with Logan and why does Joy feel a different symptom then him?

# The Beginning of the End

Authors noteShit is about to go down this chapter ...

As I was sitting in class I still felt just a little bit shook up about the whole situation. I suggested to just go home after, but Logan insisted we needed a bit of normalcy and try to enjoy the normal moments before the virus gets too out of hand and we won't even be seeing each other in person anymore.

But my problem is with Dr. Whittaker. What's his plan? What does he want with us? And why does this whole situation just seem off? Very clearly something is off-putting about him and not just his looks. He's just seems so empty it's like only the darkest thoughts shine through out his head. The way he stares, the way he stands, they way he looks and me and Logan as new toys to play with scares me honestly.

I look up and realize that the teacher has already walked in and is starting a lesson. Everyone was quiet and listening as I didn't even notice the teacher in the classroom. I groan silently resting my head down on the desk. I need to calm myself down.

I feel something on my hand and I see Logan put his hand on top of mine rubbing his thumb smoothly across it. I start to feel goosebumps along my body and feel my face heat up at the small gesture. I look up at him to see him not looking at me, but mindlessly paying attention to the teacher. I go to put my other hand on top of his but I realize something is wrong with his hand. He seems to have 2 small dark blueish black patches next to each other. I scrunch my eyes in confusion before I tap him to get his attention. He looks down at me with a small smile not even realizing what's going on.

"What's on your hand?" I ask. He looks down and his eyes widen. He lets go of my hand and holds his hand up to his face then analyzes some more to find some on his left arm.

"I have no clue." He says looking at them in disbelief.

I start to get worried. If he doesn't know what it is then what is it? I look closer at the patches and start to realize they look like the vaccine- wait, is this a side effect from the cure? What if by the end of this side effect he looks like a giant, six-two, blue monster.

"Do you think it's a side effect? Maybe others have them too." I say nervously as his arms began to shake slightly. I can obviously tell that he is very much concerned and scared as I am, but won't show it.

I grab his hands and bring them down to his lap starting to get nervous. What if Dr. Whittaker was telling the truth and this was another part of his episodes and its worse this time. I can't risk anything worser happening to Logan. I don't know how to stop it and I am not an expert on this. The last thing I want to do is see Dr. Whittaker, but from what I'm seeing we don't have a choice.-

Next week

After talking to Logan about his condition I slowly convinced him that we should see Dr. Whittaker. The patches on his skin were abnormal and no other person seemed to have it. We were going to see him the next day after we got our first vaccine like instructed, but there was no sign of him or any of the doctors. The school then announced that they will be back next week to give us the next shot since they were busy giving shots out to other schools. I got worried that Logan was going to have another episode during the week, but to our surprise nothing happened, thankfully, but the world around us on the other hand, seemed to be falling apart.

They put out curfews saying that you have to be 21 or older to be out after 9:45pm, but only for medical reasons. If you needed something after 9:45 you would have to call the police for help and even that didn't help since they were so busy dealing with other problems. Not to mention people got sicker even after they took the cure. The government stated that even if you took the first vaccine and became violently ill, not to take the second one because your sickness will get worse like my dad.

My father came home a couple days ago barely able to stand and claimed to be was having symptoms of the virus. Because of this he has been put to bed rest until cleared by a doctor. My sisters and I go to check on him every few hours to make sure he is alright, but I can see his health declining. It was a scary sight to see especially because I already lost my mother.

Due to all the sick people, the government is trying to minimalize contact so they shut down the school and basically the rest of world. Since we weren't allowed back to school I was worried Logan would never get the chance to get the second shot and he would be getting an episode, but today all my worries cleared as they allowed us to go back to school for a few hours to take the second shot.

"Hey Dad." I say entering his room to see his frail, sick body underneath the covers. "Today we all have to take the second shot of the vaccine. Me and the girls have to go to our school for a couple hours and then we'll be back."

He looks up acknowledging me shaking his head weakly. He goes to speak but stops as a loud cough erupts from his throat. I get closer to him to make him feel better by giving him a sip of water that is by his half eaten plate on the side of his bed. I feel the strings of my heart pull as I stare at the sickly man on the bed. The man that was one filled with health and bright brown skin that has now been turned a pale-ish brown red, with the rash throughout his whole body. I kiss the top of his forehead and pull the covers up more.

"I'll see you after school dad." With that I walk out the door with unshed tears in my eyes. I go to my sister's room wiping the tears telling them it's time to leave. I look down at my phone and see a message that Logan is outside waiting for us.

My sisters and I leave the house telling my dad bye one last time before I see Logan and his siblings in the car. I sit in the back seat with the kids as Luke was driving and Logan was in the front seat with him. My sisters go to the same school as Logan's so we only have to make 1 stop before going to our school.

"Hey, good morning." I say as I sat comfortably in the car.

"Good morning." Logan and Luke both reply at the same time.

We do some small talk before I look out of my window looking at the scenery of the world. Everyday so far has been grey, dull, and boring. The sky doesn't shine as much as it used to the plants look to be withering away with the rest of the world. I sigh deeply resting my head on my hand listening to the background music playing on the radio. I look down on my leg when I feel a vibration from my phone. I look down to see a message from Logan.

Logan-How are you holding up

Me-I'm good just hoping for the best, you know?

Logan-Is Megan still ignoring you?

I groan internally as I remember the Megan problem. Ever since that day we took the shot I have not heard a single word from her. It's like she has disappeared. I tried calling her, texting, I even went over to her house just to find no one. No need to say I was getting pissed. Soon after I just gave up on the texting and calling and will wait for her to show up when she does.

Me-No I'm pretty sure she is avoiding me and doesn't wanna see me.

Logan-I'm sorry I hope it gets better. And tell your dad I said hi and hopes he gets better

Me-Will do

I turn off my phone leaning back in my seat until I see my Mya, Octavia, and Lily's school. Me and Logan walk them to the front of the school telling them that we will pick them up in about 3 hours and to be safe. Soon after we dropped them off we arrived to our school that is packed with some students in masks, other wearing gloves, and I'm pretty sure I just saw someone was with a safety hazard suit. I open the car door and before I close it I thank Luke.

"Thanks for dropping us off see you soon." I say grabbing my backpack slinging it over my arms.

"Yep. No problem." Luke said giving me a small grin. I grab Logan's hand and began walking inside the building.

"You think we will be alright? I seen someone with a safety hazard suit, we don't even have masks on."

Logan chuckles a bit at my nervousness before saying "Yes, I'm pretty sure we will be fine we are about to take the 2nd shot right now, so even if we get sick we should be alright." I nod my head in agreement, we should be fine but my overthinking gets to me a lot more than I should let it. I want us to be okay, I want my family to be okay, and I just want all of this to go back normal I really hope we take this cure and that is the end of it.

Logan and I make our way to the normal lines again as we aren't going in those backrooms. We both decided that we are safer out her infront of everyone else rather in that tiny room with a few people. As we are in the lines again I lay back and put my head against the wall behind me.I close my eyes for a second until I open them again and see Logan in the corner of my eye looking at me concerned.

"Hey you good?" He asks.

"Yeah, just kinda sad and stressed, mostly sad though." I reply back

"Are you sad about your dad and Megan?" He asks knowingly

"Yes, you know I am. I just really want better things happening for all of us. Like what kind of world are we living in. Like have you noticed that the Earth has been looking so dull lately, it's like someone just took color from the sky away and I happen to really like the sky! And it is not even just that things aren't getting better, they seem to just keep getting worser and worser every minute. I feel like I'm living in some type of dystopian movie where this is the end of the world." I say releasing all of my frustrations.

I was expecting to look up and find him staring at me like I am crazy, but it was actually the opposite. Logan is looking down at me with caring eyes and admiration.

"I believe evrything will work out for the greater good, Joy. You have to stop feeling so scared all the time and learn to see the brighter side of things. Yes Megan may be gone, and your dad is very sick, but they are still here. Also you know Megan often leaves when things get inconvient, she is fine, your dad is fine, and you most importantly are fine." Logan finishes with an encouraging smile on his face. This is why I fell in love with him. He has always been so positive despite all the bad going around, and I can't lie it does make me feel better.

"You really think we are going to be fine?" I ask one last time for my reassurance.

"Yes Joy, I believe we will."

I give him a very big smile before resting my head on his shoulder. I felt much better until I looked at his neck and seen multiple small patches that are dark blue again. I wasn't going to say anything because he had been getting more ever since he hasn't taken the 2nd shot, but he has them trailing down his neck all the way to his hand.

"Logan why the hell do you have so many more patches, you didnt have this much before." I say analyzing his arm. Logan looks down and realizes that he actually does has so many more patches.

"I'm not sure there wasnt as many patches when I woke up this morning" he said looking at his hands. I look at his hands as well and realize that there is a patch forming on his hand right in front of my face. I quickly get his attention by tapping him

"Logan what the hell, look at your hand, there is a patch appearing right now." I say in panic. He goes to look at his hand before he starts coughing real bad, but what got my attention was the blood in his hand after coughing. I start pushing everyone out the line and grab Logan with me to go to the front of the line. I look at the doctor that is in the front of the line and frantically point to Logan. Then out of the corner of my eyes I see Dr. Whittaker and Lindsey rushing to where we are at.

"What is going on." Lindsey says while immediately taking Logan inside. I wanted to ask why they decided to come all the way over to us, but held back as Logan could possibly die.

"I don't know. Shouldn't you guys know? He just started coughing out of no where and he has these weird patches over his body, look!" I say out in a rush while Lindsey rushes and comes back with 2 different needles, one with the same blue, black liquid and the other is just a plain white clear liquid. She injects him with the clear liquid needle and suddenly Logan stops coughing and sits up straight, he breaths in heavily and is panting really hard.

I release a breath I have been keeping in and kneel down to the chair that Logan was sitting in holding his face. I look up a Dr. Whittaker not taking anymore bullshit. "Dr. Whittaker what is happening with him" I say yelling at him

"I did say he would have another episode did I not?" He says in his same monotone voice.

"You never said he was going to have these weird patches over his body or that he would be coughing up blood, did you not?" I say right back.

"No you are correct, but I did say it wasn't going to be pretty." He says this time with a hint of playfulness. I glare my eyes dead at him with pure hatred. We cannot come back here again. Me and Logan are done and I don't even care anymore if I get sick. This has gone entirely too far.

"You know what we are done here! I no longer want to play whatever game you have with us. Forget this vaccine, forget all of the doctors in here lying to us, and forget you Dr. Whittaker because you need serious help. Everything that you do is beyond creepy and I have a feeling you know it, you are a sick man and I want to be part of it no more!" I say almost yelling at the end of my sentence. I pull up Logan ready to leave this room as of right now until Dr. Whittaker slowly looks at me and just smiles.

I start to feel very uneasy and look away from him. He shakes his head while laughing and then he stops abruptly. He looks me dead in the eye, straight at me. "Oh sweetheart you simply don't understand." he says pointing at Logan. I look at Logan to see what he is pointing at until I feel a familiar sensation in my arm. I look down and notice Lindsey has put a needle in me with the 2nd dose. I start to panic even more, and was about to go off until I feel a sharp pain hit throughout my body.

I fall on the ground screaming at the top of my lungs. The pain was too much. Every cell in my body was being lit on fire and a knife felt like it was being sliced into my every part of my skin, I look down as I felt something moving through my arms, and see my veins in my arms and hands were glowing black and dark blue-ish that is glittery. I was so caught up in my own pain to realize that Logan was on the floor, and everyone in that room was on the floor as well crying for help.

I crawl on my legs slowly through the pain that was in my body and try to get closer to Logan. I held his hand while crying in pain on the floor, until with my own 2 eyes I see Logan changing, changing into something I have never seen before.

The dark patches on his skin has now expanded all over his body. His plain white teeth has now turned into sharp razor pointy teeth, and he body was cracking and breaking in every place you can think of. His clothes ripped from his body as they scattered around the floor. I look up at him in horror and realize his face isn't him anymore. All the hair that once been on his head has, now been onto the floor and he's shaking, shaking so uncontrollably. I start to back up on my knees as I see that he's growing bigger and bigger. I look around and see that people are staring up at him.

The room that was once filled with the cries of our pain have now turned into cries of help and desperation.

Logan stops shaking and looks at Dr. Whittaker with those cold dark blue eyes. He charges over there and lifts him up by his neck and throws him across the room. Everyone painfully gets off the floor and runs to leave the room, seeing that Logan has gone crazy. Logan marches over to where he threw Dr. Whittaker, I slowly limp over their tears in my eyes, my hand over my stomach to try to stop him.

Surprisingly I can easily turn Logan around with one of my hands and pull him to look right into his eyes.

"Logan." I say whispering.

# The Beginning of The End Part 2

I look around the room to see people still in pain trying to get away from the monster they see with their own 2 eyes. The room is so loud and my head and body is pounding like cars crashing into each other. All I can think of is that we have to leave now.

I swallow hard as I look into Logan's eyes. "Hey Logan, baby it's okay we gotta go ok? We gotta leave now"I say with a lump in my throat, sweat dripping down my neck. I was praying to God that he would listen. My body was still in so much pain and I could barely get myself to say those words to him.

He looks at Dr. Whittaker for a minute squinting his eyes for a bit before he looks back at me realizing how much pain I'm really in. He kicks Dr. Whittaker in his stomach and he starts to groan with blood dripping down the side of his head and mouth.

Logan picks me up bridal style and carries me out the room. My eyes could barely open as I see Logan's silhouette carrying me out towards the exit. I desperately hold on to his arms to keep me from falling out of them. As I touched his arm it felt as if I was touching the hard, cold, rough floor. His arm felt like a fucking floor?! I almost would've passed out if I already on the brink of it.

People move out the way as they see Logan walking shaking the ground with each movement. One girl looks right at him, she looks like she seen someone die and come back to life. She held her hand close to her chest as she opened her mouth and let out a blood curling scream. The scream was so intense it had us on the floor holding our ears trying to stop the sound from flowing into our ears.

Everyone goes back to thrashing on the floor screaming, in yet again more pain. I tried to hold on to Logan to keep my hand wrapped around his arm so I don't lose him but her screams were so loud and deafening I had to put my hands on my ears. It felt as if sharp needles were pricking my ear drums going deeper each prick. I look at Logan doing the same as I am but he keeps trying to get back up, but falling each time.

Hearing loud blasting noises behind us, I turn my head to the see people with lab coats having these weird, metal shaped objects that look to be shooting blurs of blue light from it. I see them shooting down the teenagers trying to get them to calm down but the students using their new found abilities keep fighting back. If then wasn't the time to leave, now most definitely was. Turning back to the girl who's still screaming, I try to get her to stop.

My ears were bleeding at this point and so were everyone else's. I crawl to the best of my ability towards her and try to scream over her loud pitch screaming, but to no avail it didn't work. I try getting closer again seeing as the lab coats were still getting moving towards us, but she wouldnt stop staring at Logan in fear. I had about enough when I start to feel this rush of power flow through me. I don't know if it was out of fear, anger, and me just being annoyed by this girl but I just needed her to shut up! And then thats exactly what she did.

She was choking on air grasping around her throat with eyes wide. She finally was quiet. I stared at her longer daring her to try and open her mouth again. Her face was nearly blue and I wanted it to stay that way, so she did. I glared at her just a little longer until I see her choking up on her own blood. The red liquid fell out of her mouth onto the cold floor. I jump back to reality after seeing the blood and she let in a huge breath, gasping to get the air she missed.

I raised my eyebrows in confusion as if I meant to do that or not. I jump a bit when I see my blood coming from me hit the floor. I touch my nose and see red on my fingers as I pulled back. Logan seems to have come back to reality as we hear the lab coats coming dangerously close to us. He jumped off the floor and grabbed me into his arms again as we ran down the hallways.

More gasps where heard as we flew pass people as they look to see a big, black, 8 foot monster run around with me in his arms. People were already running but if they weren't running before they sure as hell are running now.

I look behind him and I see people running not to far behind us with suits on and equipment in their hands. They werent the people with the lab coats but they had the same weird weapon again, but they also had these little mechanical balls that had the same light blue, energy coming from it. I couldn't see that well, but they were throwing it directly at us, well maybe just Logan as he is the abnormally large creature.

I shake his arm as hard as I can while pointing to behind us trying to signal him what was happening. "L- Logan," I say trying to stay conscious "look behind us they're trying to hurt you." Logan starts to run much more faster then what he was already.

Not to say I haven't been confused this whole time, but he just made it worst. We are literally passing everyone in the hallways like he's the flash or some shit. I held on to him tighter scared that I was gonna fall down. I feel myself slipping in and out of conscious. I try to stay awake to the best of my ability, but my body just felt so weak. I can feel Logan wrap his rough arms around me holding me tighter

I look up at him and trying not to close my eyes. Now I know I was falling in and out of consciousness but I know I didn't see his lips move, but I heard his voice. "Stay with me Joy. Dammit Joy are you fucking listening stay with me please." He says, or thinks to me I dont really know anymore as I couldn't open my eyes any longer. I felt the darkness pull me in and i accepted it. I didnt wanna give up but my body couldnt take it.

"Fuck!" is all I hear before I felt the blackness hit me.-------

# *Powers?*

I felt something warm being pressed on my head. I want to open my eyes but the room felt to bright. I slowly open my eyes, putting my hands up so that I don't get to overwhelmed by the brightness.

I look between the fingers on my hand and saw Lindsey and Dr. Whittaker above me with a wet rag on my forehead. I scoot back on the soft cushion I was placed on and close my eyes putting my knees up against my while holding onto my shirt.

I start to scream and hyperventilate. This cant be happening right now, it's not happening right now. I shake my head back and forth and hold my legs close to my chest whimpering and whispering to protect myself.

"No, no no no no no no no NO" I whisper, sweat dripping down my face. I open my eyes to see Dr. Whittaker walk towards me with a syringe and a smile splattered across his face. I feel someone shaking my arms and I start to get more scared.

"Get the fuck away from me! Stay away, please" I say going back to closing my eyes. I start to feel the room shaking. I put my fingers to my ears making sure my eyes are closed shut. I dont want to go with him, I want to leave, I cant stay here. I start to feel the room shaking more rapidly.

"Joy, Joy, Joy!" I hear a voice speak up, it sounded like Logan. I slowly let go of my ears and open my eyes. I look up I see a worried Logan staring in front of me. This time he's not in his monster form, but in his plain old Logan form and he has all his hair, with too small clothes on. I see more people behind Logan to find his younger sister and older brother looking at me. I then look around my living room and see a couple of family pictures on the floor, along with vases and other things completely broken. I rub my eyes and blink a couple of times just to make sure I wasn't imagining this.

"Hey are you okay?" Logan says holding me by my shoulders. I look at him and squint my eyes one more time to make sure I wasnt tripping.

"Logan are you actually here?" I say wanted to believe he is here. He chuckles lightly.

"Yeah, I'm here." He hugs me and pull into his embrace. I accept happily and hold him tightly to me.

"Did I do this...? " I say pulling back from Logan looking at the now messy living room.

"I'm pretty sure you did." I hear Logan say a bit suprised.

As I was going to respond I see my younger sisters run up to me. I feel 2 pairs of arms wrap around me and big doe eyes look up at me with a small smile.

"We missed you Joy!" Mya says."Yeah we were scared when people started going crazy" my other sister Octavia said. I break away from the hug and look at them with my eyebrows scrunched.

"What happened to you guys? Are you guys hurt?!" I ask frantically inspecting their small bodies. They nod their heads.

"Yes Joy we are ok, but we wanna show you something." I slowly let go of their bodies while looking back at Logan wondering if he knows what is about to happen. He only shrugs his shoulder looking just as confused with me.

I set my gaze back upon the twins as they hold one of their hands together and they lift the opposite hand out in front of them. I raise my eyebrow intrigued by what is going to happen and then I see a dark firey red emit from Mya's hand and a dark icy blue that seemed to have little crystallized snowflakes coming out of Octavia like flows of energy.

I look up at everyone in the room confused. Not to say that I've been feeling that emotion quite a lot today as well, but I then see the twins put up their hands in my direction and I felt a gush of coldness come towards me I see my hands started to turn blue with an icy sheet covering my hand and become frozen. I start to freak out as I feel the numbness of my hands. They feel like they are about to fall off until I felt a hot heat that melted away the ice sheet off of me.

It took me a minute to undertsand what just happened. I would be happy if under certain circumstances (because powers are f- ing cool) but this feels anything else but cool. One minute we are at school getting vaccines, the next we are all superheros where even the dangerous of all people can have extraordinary powers. Imagine if a crazy serial killer had the powers that my sisters possessed or some other weird powers that could not just put us, but the whole world in danger. It dawned upon me that we are totally screwed right now and these powers are about to be the main cause if it. Conflicted would be the best word to expain this situation as of right now.

After realizing I was staring at my hands in shock without giving anyone a reaction about what just happened I feel Logan grab my face in the palms of his hands. Gently rubbing my cheeks with the stroke of his thumb as he speaks up.

"Are you okay Joy? I know this may seem all confusing right now, but I want you to know that whatever happens from here that I will protect you and your family. We will figure this out and we will be alright, ok."

I was going to ask how the hell will he protect us from whatever is going on, but I did realize he turned into an 8 foot creature. I look at Logan again, but this time in a new light, or darkness I suppose. He turned into a creature. A dark, spiky, razor sharp creature at that. It was nothing like I've ever seen before. The fear was still very prominent, but knowing that the creature was Logan made me feel a tad less scared. Seeing as I was eyeballing him he puts his head down knowing what I'm going to ask him.

"Yes Joy it was me, I was the monster." I can see the strained look in his eyes as he spoke those words. He seemed as if being that creature made him vile, disgusted, and most definitely ashamed.

I reach over to him and put my hands on his face like he did.

"You aren't a monster Logan and you never will be." I state assuring him that him having this ability doesn't make him any less of the sweet, caring Logan that I know. He holds my hand rubbing his thumb across it.

"Those people who were trying to shoot you down, what happened to them?" I ask remembering the events prior to this.

He removes his hand from mine as I drop them to the sides of me. "I don't really know, but we were gone before they could catch up to us. Then I went over to my house to find Luke with the girls and we brung them over here to check up on your dad."

"Is my dad ok, his condition hasn't gotten worse right?" I ask hoping that he was just as fine as where I left him this morning.

He looks up unsure what to say and my heart drops. "What? What's wrong with him?!"

"We are pretty sure he is in a coma right now. He wasn't responsive when we were trying waking him up. He just laid flat with his eyes shut no matter how much noise we made or how hard we shook him." He says looking up at me with sadness filled in his eyes. As he spoke those words I start to feel my legs give out. I move slowly towards the couch sitting while holding my chest. Just as I thought this day couldn't get any worse. I see a glass of water in front of me as I look up and see Luke alongside Lily with a sad smile.

He sits next to me patting my back in a fatherly manner.

"Thank you Luke." I say in a small voice taking a sip of my water. Lily comes and sits on Luke's lap while waving at me shyly.

"Hi Lily." I say pinching her cheek lightly like I usually do. She gives me a simple smile that doesn't reach her eyes that it normally would.

Still patting my back gently Luke speaks up. "Do you want to go see your dad?" He asks in a very soft voice.

"No." I reply quickly. A little to quickly because Logan looks at me with his eyebrows raised.

"It's just that I don't want to see him in that condition right now. I need some time to breath." I say truthfully. I couldn't see him right now even if I wanted to. I would feel broken if I went upstairs and saw his body that seemed lifeless. I already lost my mother, and I'm definitely not ready to lose him.

"Okay that's fine take your time." Luke says trying to calm things down.

"So do you guys have any abilities?" I ask trying to change the topic.

"No I do not, but we think Lily might. She hasn't been speaking probably due to shock." He says rubbing the top of her head. Lily only looks sadly at me and bows her head down. I instantly feel sympathy for the young girl. She's to little to have this type of trauma.

I nod my head understandingly and look back to Logan ready for more answers.

"So what's going to happen now?"

"Well if you mean what's happening in the world, the government has stated that this is a national issue and that other countries who have taken this cure are also very much going through the same thing. They internet is down, but they are giving us instructions on any screen that's electronic with using whatever backup internet they have." Logan explains to me.

"So what did the government say about these powers?" I ask wondering what's happening to everyone else."

"They said that if you have abilities please go to the place where you got the vaccine and everyone else needs to stay inside and lock their door. We are instructed not to leave until they upload a new update."

"We aren't going back to the school right?" I ask knowing the reason we are at home and not school is probably because we don't trust what's going on over there.

Logan looks at me with a knowing look. "Yes we aren't going back because we don't trust the school or Dr. Whittaker to do the right thing. We are going to stay here until we know exactly what are plan is, since it doesn't seem like we are going to have our normal lives back."

I nod my head knowing that's that is probably true. We aren't going to get our lives back. Who knows what's going to happen after this or if we will even make it out of whatever this is.

All of a sudden I feel a sharp rush of nerves crawl up my back. My body instantly goes into alert mode. I stand up from the couch looking to Logan to see if he feels this too, but he is already staring at the door.

"Logan who do you think is out ther-" I try to say but he shushed me.

I look at Luke and could tell that he is very confused as to what's going on.

"I feel someone at the door we need to go to the upstairs now!" I say to everyone urgently. The person at the door seems to be very conflicted and troubled. Their scent reeks of full of anxiety and fear. They seem to have a powerful aura radiating around them, which could mean their powers are extra strong. I would be questioning how I can feel that, but I'm more focused on as to why would they be coming to MY door at this time. Everyone should be in their houses locked safe away from the dangers outside. So what is this person doing?

"Joy, go upstairs with the Luke and the kids I'm going to see who is at this door." Logan says in a protective stance waiting for whoever is outside the door to come inside.

Luke tries to pulls Logan back, but Logan doesn't budge a bit.

"I'M the older brother I will check who is at the door, not you." Luke says trying to protect him older brother.

"And I am much stronger now and can protect you. You need to go upstairs before you get hurt Luke." Logan says back to him with no room for arguing.

I was going to try to get their attention, because there is danger outside and there is no time for arguing, until the presence out there felt familiar, like a good familiar. I see Logan and Luke still bickering but then Logan looks right at me telling me with his eyes to go upstairs, but it's just something about that presence that feels so normal that I don't feel any danger. I walk up to the door to go open it.

I can feel everyone's eyes on my staring at me like I'm crazy. I see Logan try to grab my arm and stop me but I already opened the door before he could.

"Megan?" -----------Fun fact I forgot to make the twins names and went back into earlier chapters to give them a name

# The End Fall

"Megan?!" I ask softly hoping that it's really her. I grab her and pull her inside while hugging her close with tears threatening to spill out my eyes. I hear her light crying as she grabbed on to me tightly.

Out the corner of my eye I see everyone in the room visibly relax. Megan and I stay holding each other close before I pull back waiting for her to start talking.

"Um so I can't really explain right now. But I know one thing is that we can't stay here for long." She says quietly. What? THAT'S the first thing she tells me.

"What do you mean? What aren't you telling me Megan?"

I see her contemplating whether or not she should tell me before she speaks up again. "We really need to go. Like we should leave now." Her tone sounds freakishly calm, but the words she said are anything but calm.

I scrunch my eyebrow not trusting her words. Does it really matter if we stay or leave? We are in more danger out there. She looks up at me then speaks the words right out head.

"We need to go because as a matter of fact we are safer out there than we are in here." I squint my eyes wondering if I accidently said that outloud.

"No you didn't say that out loud."

Can she read minds?!

"Yes I can as a matter of fact." I flick my head so hard at her. Did I hear correctly or did she just say she can read my mind?

"Yes I did Joy- look if you're going to keep being surprised can you do it when we are somewhere safer." She begs with a worried look.

I see that Logan looks a bit confused at our conversation before he connects the pieces. "You can read minds, huh." He states as a fact.

"Yes and I can hear you thinking if I know you were the creature roaming at school, that I overhead the government is trying their hardest to pinpoint. I didn't know, but thanks for the heads up momster boy" Megan says standing walking towards him.

"That is also more the reason as why we need to leave. Now." She says crossing her arms

If Megan can read minds then she probably knows exactly what the danger is and is trying to protect us from it by not telling us. I'm still very reluctant to leave especially if people are out looking for Logan, but Megan came back. She came back just to warn us about the danger, she's risking everything to help us.

"Ok we should go Logan. She can read minds. She's trying to protect us right now. We should listen to her." I say trying to reason with him. He looks at Megan then back at me.

"Alright I trust your judgment let's go." I nod my head thankful that he decided to listen.

"Ok everyone pack as much as we can take in the car, don't bring any useless things. Meet back here in 45 minutes."

"Make it 30, we should be leaving right now." Megan says cutting me off from what I was saying.

"Well 30 minutes I guess. Hurry now." I say as everyone starts getting their things. Luke, Lily, and Logan all rush outside to their house. I rush upstairs helping Mya and Octavia gather all their things. I grab some of my stuff before I enter my dad's room. I go up to him hoping he's not actually in a coma. I reach for his hands feeling the rough calloused palms. He lays still, not even moving once as I touch him. I feel a lone tear fall down my face.

What if this is the last of him and thats how I remember him as he withers away. I couldn't lose him, he's a part of me. He raised, cherished, and loved me. If he passes he remembers me as his little girl, while I only remember him drifting away losing more and more of himself by day. He doesn't even know what's going on to the world around him as he lays here peaceful as ever.

I wipe the tear from my face packing some of his things in a suitcase before gently picking him up. I don't know if it's my newfound powers or the fact he hasn't been eating that much, but he really is light to pick up. I carry him and some of our bags downstairs meeting with everyone else. They all looked shock to see me carrying my father in one hand and a couple of suitcases in the other.

"So what exactly would your power be?" Luke asks what I'm pretty sure everyone is thinking.

"I'm not really sure but-" I get cut off by Megan.

"Yeah no time for chitchat let's leave now please." She states grabbing all her things running outside to my dad's car. We all rush outside with her, until I realize I forgot the keys.

"Wait I forgot the keys!" I say handing my stuff and my dad to Logan before I rush inside. But as I'm looking for his keys I feel a multiple presences at the back door and they presence screamed hostile.

"Copy, sir do I have permission to go inside the house. We think the monster and the young girl is in there, copy." I hear whoever is outside whisper into his walkie talkie. I wouldn't have heard it without this superhearing I assume I have, but grateful that I have it as it just helped me a lot. I look and see the keys on the counter right next to the back door. I slowly make my way over there trying to grab it quickly, but I jump back as they kicked the door down. I see a handful of soldiers walk in with guns.

I grab the keys fast trying to move back as quick as I can before the soldier who spoke in the walkie talkie spoke up. "Drop the keys and bend on your knees with your hands behind your head." He yells at me with a southern accent. I flinch a bit not doing anything he just told me. "Now girl or I'll shoot ya!" He barks back at me. I close my eyes shaking my head wishing I could be outside right now.

I feel that rush of adrenaline come over my body again, and I open my eyes as I'm back outside infront with everyone else. I look around in shock. I turn my back towards everyone trying to warn them, but that was short-lived as I heard 3 loud gun shots shoot outside the front door.

"GO NOW!" I yell at everyone to get in the car. I start running while I tossed the keys to Luke and ran to the back seat. I grab the twi.ns and Lily shoving them in the back with me as Logan gets in with us holding my dad over his shoulder. The soldiers run out the front door shooting at the car.

"Step out of the vehicle and no one will get hurt!" The soldier yells

"Luke start the fucking car now!" Logan screams ignoring the soldiers warning. We all duck down in the back seat as Luke is trying to not get shot struggling to put the key into the ignition. Megan takes it away from him and turns it on.

"Hurry and drive." She stares at him deadly.

Luke shakily puts the car in reverse, driving off as the soldiers shoot trying to hit the tires. He speeds through the streets as I heard the soldier speak in his walkie talkie again.

"Dammit! Copy they got away. Copy I repeat they got away copy." He yells frustrated.

I slowly lift my head up and unwrap my arms from my crying sisters. "Is everyone alright?" I ask looking around to see if anyone got hurt.

Everyone shakes their head signaling they are fine. I take in a huge breath as I take account the absolute danger we are in. How are we supposed to manage now? We have no parental guidance to help us, just these powers that we can't seem to figure out and a team of soldiers trying to murder us. We literally just got shot at, we need to figure something out and figure it out fast.

"That was close. Way too close. Next time we say drive Luke, we fucking mean it. There's no time to be shaken up or scared! We could've died!" Megan says yelling at Luke.

"I know, I know. I've jus- Fuck! I've never been in a situation like this. I mean this is insane you guys." Luke says running one of his hands through his hair.

"Yeah well neither have we, yet we still have to-" She gets cut off by Logan.

"Give him a fucking break Megan. How is he supposed to react to this? How are any of us supposed to react to this really! Shit happens, we're human. He got scared, it won't happen again." He says sitting back in his seat glaring at Megan.

"Well you aren't even human anymore, are you Logan?" I see Logan's face instantly turn up. He looks like he is ready to punch someone. I speak up before this can escalate any farther.

"Megan that was uncalled for. Look we are all in this fucked up situation, okay. We have no clue what to do and how to act. No one prepares themselves for these type of situations, so we shouldn't be judging each other on how we do respond to them. That being said we need to suck it up and stop arguing with each over dumb things. Alright?" I finish speaking as I see Megan roll her eyes crossing her arm around her chest.

"Whatever." She says mumbling lowly.

"Thank you Joy. I'm sorry everyone, I know I put everyone at risk, but it won't happen again." He says speaking up still shaken about what just happened.

"But the real question is what are we going to do?" He speaks again.

"Funny how the only adult here conscious is asking a bunch of teens what to do." Megan barks back.

"You guys are the ones with powers so, yes I'm looking to you guys for answers." Luke replies softly.

"Well one thing I know for sure right now is to hope that things get better." Logan says staring out the window sighing loudly.

"Very sweet Logan, but I think your brother meant was an actual plan. Not blinded hope." Megan said sarcastically.

"Enough Megan just tell us where are going." I say tired of not just her attitude, but everything else.

She grumbles under her breath a bit before replying.

"A place I go to when I need to be alone."-

While driving everyone was pretty quiet after their little arguments. The roads weren't filled with many people as we passed by a few cars. Soon we pull up into this abandon store, that apparently Megan goes to when she needs a break from the world. So this is where she goes when I can't find her.

"Yeah, it's a comfort spot and it's hidden from everyone else." She replies mindlessly.

I really need to keep my thoughts in control.

"Pull around to the side, there is some storage space that should be big enough to hold the car in. I'm going to go inside and open it." She says getting out the car running inside the building. Luke goes where Megan instructed him to and we see Megan opening the storage that looked like a garage and had a few boxes and other random things. He pulls inside hitting some of the boxes before turning the car off.

I grab my now sleeping sisters while Logan grabs my dad, and Luke holds Lily. Megan takes us through the abandoned store where we keep walking to what seemed to be a basement. She opens the door and we walk down the steps. As I look in the basement it looks dingy and sort of dark. There is a light bulb on the ceiling that has a metal light string that she pulls to turn on. I then look at the floor and see that there is a little makeshift bed along with open snacks and magazines surrounding it. There wasn't really much around the room other then boxes stacked on each other.

I look around the room in awe. This is really where Megan stays at. All the times I went looking for her worried sick, hoping that she was okay and here she was, snacking on food in a basement or an abandoned store. Not that I'm mad, because it was way better than what I was thinking she was doing.

"Ok we will sleep here until we can figure out our next step. We are going to stay low hoping that they don't find us." Megan explains to us. We nod our heads putting everyone down and unpacking our things. We all make our little makeshift beds putting our sisters comfortably next to each other.

I stand up stretching my back as I feel my stomach rumble. "What are we going to eat Megan?" I ask needing at least a snack. She turns around to one of the boxes in the corner before pulling out some canned food and chips.

"I don't know when this store went out of business, but they have stale snacks and some canned food in these boxes." She says tossing them over to me. I look down at the can that had spaghetti on it. I sit down on the floor while opening it up. I then start to eat it with my hand, not caring how I look. It did taste gross not being heated up, but nothing that I couldn't handle. I start putting the can to my mouth, like I was it was a drink and slurp it up. I lick my lips while I start opening up the chips. I bit into the stale potato chips while I look up at everyone who is staring at me.

"What?" I ask with my mouth full.

"Nothing you just looks a tad bit.."

"Animalistic. " Megan blandly says finishing off for Logan.

"I would've used a nicer word, but yeah. Did you eat at all today?" Logan asks sitting next to me taking some of the potato chips out the bag. I recall back to this morning as I thought it was going to be a normal day. I ate a normal breakfast today so I shouldn't be hungry, but for some reason I felt like I could eat a whole buffet right now.

"Yes, but I am really hungry right now." I say shoving the rest of the chips in my mouth crumbling up the bag before tossing it. I lick my fingers before grabbing another bag of chips and a magazine before laying next to my sisters. I see Logan shake his head before coming to lay next to me. He wraps his arm around my waist as he looks through his own magazine.

I finish eating the chips I grabbed and then look through my magazine flipping through the pages. The next thing you know I feel my eyelids getting heavy while I doze off.-

I woke up rubbing my eyes to see that it was pitch black and everyone was asleep. I feel my stomach rumble again. Damn I'm still hungry? I go to get up to get me another snack till I feel Logan squeeze me tighter. I turn to look at him just to see he's wide awake staring at the ceiling.

"Logan?" I call out to him but he doesn't respond.

"Logan." I repeat shaking him a but. He doesn't turn to me.

"Joy what do you think will happen to us?" He asks still staring mindlessly. I furrow my eyebrows wondering what does he mean.

"Logan what are you talking about?"

"I mean look at us. We are in a basement, eating stale chips, with super powers. I mean what is going to happen from here on out. Will we live in here for months until we can't stand each other? Are my parents ever going to find where we are at? Will I turn into a monster again and attack you guys? Will your powers start to get out of control? I mean what will happen from this very moment cause based on what I'm feeling, we're trapped." He finishes turning his body to me this time.

I look down at him lightly seeing his features in the dark. Logan is the one who usually has hope during these times, the optimistic one, but I see him staring at me completely hopeless. I havent thought about Logans parents as they could possibly have powers to. It also made me think about how I'm the only one with a parent right now, yes h's in a coma, but nonethelesshes still here. I reach out to him to try and bring comfort until I feel goosebumps race down my body. Someone's here. By the looks of it Logan feels it too as his eyes widen. We quickly sit up from the floor quietly waking everyone up. I go to Megan shaking her rapidly.

"Megan get up now!" I whisper yell frantically. She stirs a little bit before she stares up at me.

"Joy what? What's wron-" She stops speaking looking around the dark room. I'm assuming she could feel the multiple presences above us.

"Who's here?!" She questions sitting up more alert.

"That's what we don't know. Get up now we have to leave. Is there another way out the place than upstairs?" I ask gathering even less of my things and my sisters who are being woken from the noises. I see my sisters and Lily groggily look around wondering what is happening. I grab their arms rushing them to stand up, and then I grab my dad carefully putting him over my shoulders.

"Yeah if we move the boxes there should be a door-" She gets cut off as the door to the basement gets thrown off its hinges.

"Move now!" I hear Logan yell at everyone. We all rush to were Megan is removing the boxes from the door. She seems to be struggling so me and Logan easily push the boxes to the ground trying to open the door. We shake the door handle as it won't open. I twist it harder, but the handle breaks off.

"Fuck!" I scream tears running down my face. I start kicking the door in hopes it will break through, but just as I start kicking it I hear a familiar voice speak up.

"Well, well, well. If it ain't Ms. Pierre and Mr. Jackson." He says laughing like he isn't about to kill us. I go to kick the door again but he stops me.

"Stop trying to kick that door down Joy. I'm not gonna hurt yall if you will all cooperate." He says taking slow steps towards us. I look behind him and see multiple soldiers plus the one who was shooting at us earlier. They have flashlights gleaming at us making me squint my eyes, and this time instead of guns they have those weird weapons that blast blue light.

"Just come over here Joy, all of you actually. I want to see my lovely creations." He says with a grin plastered on his face. I gulp lightly pulling the girls behind me. I'll be damned if he's taking us without a fight. I turn to Megan hoping that she is reading my mind right now about fighting, but instead I find her holding her head twitching.

"Megan? Megan what's going on." I say reaching for her.

"Aw yes, little miss Megan. The one who lead me here." He says still grinning evilly. I turn my head at that hoping I was hearing his words right. I look at Logan who is still in a fighting stance ready to get to work. I turn back to Megan wishing that she would answer me.

"No! No you were not supposed to follow me here! I directed you to another place!" Megan says holding her head, while spit flies from her mouth. She manically shakes her head grasping her hands into her curly hair.

"Well I guess you're not as strong as you thought you were Megan. You should be aware of how weak your brain is when sleeping. It was very easier for me to go in it." He says in a baby tone laughing wildly.

"Ok enough games get over here now and maybe I won't have to hurt you guys." He says taking another step to us. Logan steps towards him in a protective stance, breathing heavily. I go to grab his arm but he shrugs it off.

"Logan, my most beautiful creation yet. You wanna come over here for me son?" Dr. Whittaker asks not at all threatened by Logan.

"Leave now and maybe you won't have to get hurt." Logan snarls menacingly. I stand back watching this play out.

"Now is that a way to treat your maker!" Whittaker says smiling. And just like that it happened in slow motion. Logan drops to the ground shaking and in an instant his bones start popping as his hair sheds off his head and his clothes start ripping. It was just as scary as the first time, as I watch the spikes protrude from his back, with the long sharp talons. His pale skin, turned dark and scaley as Logan in all of his monster glory bends lightly as he touches to ceiling. He stares daggers into Dr. Whittaker before charging towards him snarling. And just like that the soldiers start firing. The blast seem to be doing nothing as they hut Logan and he still fights back ferociously.

Dr. Whittaker has moved out the way and starts charging towards me. I stood frozen not knowing what to do before Logan steps infront of us blocking Dr. Whittaker from us.

I look at Megan who still is on shaking her head crazily. "Megan get up, c'mon." I say grabbing her arm. We move farther away as I look back at a scared Luke.

"Luke find anything you can use as a weapon. And girls, I know this might be scary, but I need you guys to try and use your powers. We are going to try and run up those stairs and go to the car, so stay close." I say making sure they understand. They nod their heads quickly as

I see tears ready to spill out their eyes. I look back to Luke and see he grabbed a crowbar that was off in a corner somewhere. I stare back at the crowd of soldiers. Well here goes nothing.

A few soldiers come at us as they see we are trying to escape. The start shooting at us while we start ducking. I stare at one of the soldiers and feel his body coursing through mine as I try to control him. I lift my hand up and he copies me. I lift my other hand, where his hand has the weapon and I make him turn around to shoot it at the other soldiers. The other soldiers take their attention off us as they try to shoot at the soldier I commanded. We run through them staying close to each other before one of them grab Octavia by her hair.

I stop once I hear her screams. I turn around to help, but one of the soldiers pull me back. I then see Mya raises her hand shooting fire at the soldier who has Octavia. The soldiers face lit up in flames as he lets go screaming. I see his skin melting right off the bone as a char smell lingers in the room. I suddenly feel the chills again as I look and I'm behind the guard that was holding me. Thank you teleportation. I hit him in the back of the head as we continue running.

We fight off more guards with our powers, and Luke's crowbar as we race up the stairs. We run out the basement to the car. I keep running till I look around and see Megan isn't with us. I turn around quickly and look over at Megan who is still holding her head hysterically crying. I run back over to her trying to pull her but she won't budge.

"You guys have to go without me." She says standing up crying.

"No what do you mean we have to leave now Megan." I say still trying to drag her towards me. She pulls bag stumbling a bit.

"Dr. Whittaker got into my head. We are connected somehow. I can't put you guys in more danger. You have to leave me here so he doesn't find out where you are heading next." She says sniffling. I grunt in frustration hitting my head. I cannot leave Megan here. She was always there for me and I have to be there for her.

"Megan I am not listening to that bullshit. Lets leave, seriously." I say reaching towards her again but I then hear a loud roaring sound coming from the basement and heavy footsteps approaching the top. I see Logan appear with blood dripping down from him. I hear his voice in my head.

"Let's go I held them off as long as I can but they are coming."

I look back at Megan with pleading eyes.

"Please Megan, don't leave me." I say tears running down my face. I hear the soldiers approaching the top of the basement as Logan goes back to fighting.

"Joy we have no time to waste, let's go now!" Logan says to me again while ripping the head off one of the soldiers. I look back at everyone else who is waiting for what's next. I turn my attention to Megan again. She looks back at me as the soldiers are crowding where Logan is at. There is too many for him to fight of as he starts moving back as more approach.

"Go Joy. I will be fine I promise. I will find you again you just have to leave now." Megan says tears falling freely. I take quick steps towards her pulling her into a bone crushing hug.

"You better." I repeat pulling away from her quickly running towards everyone else.

"Let's go. C'mon!" I say running in the direction of the car. I turn back and see Logan running with us, but not before I see them blasting Megan to the ground. Her body falls limply as they rush to pick her up put handcuffs around her that have a blue light surrounding it like the weapons. I face to the front again crying while running.

We make our way to the car while I set my dad in the back along with the girls I make my way to the passenger seat before I look at Logan who is still in his creature form.

"What are you doing, change back and get inside." I say to him confused he shakes his head before speaking to me.

"I will run with you guys just incase their is more danger surrounding the car."

I nod my head not having time to argue. Logan opens up the garage door and Luke pulls out. We turn the car around just to see more soldiers with weapons and helicopters floating above.

"Step out the car and no one will get hurt." I hear one of the soldiers say on a megaphone. Logan charges at the soldiers, but they blast him with this extra large blaster seem to be taking an effect on him. I rush out the car running towards Logan. I get to him and see that he's back into his human form and is naked on the ground. I flip him over and he is unconscious.

"Logan, Logan please get up we need you." I say pathetically crying even more. I hear footsteps coming and I see Luke along with the girls coming out the car. I stand up protectively blocking Logan as I go into a fighting stance. I feel Luke tap me getting my attention.

"Joy we can't fight them, there's just too many." He says holding me back.

"Well I'll be damned if I don't try." I reply back taking his hands off of me ready to fight.

"Joy-" He goes to say before I hear Dr. Whittaker's voice again.

"I think you should listen to him Joy. You have no where to run." He says stepping out of the garage space and over to us. I turn around glaring at him.

"Don't be like thay Joy just come to us willingly, and I'll take good care of ya." He says rubbing his beard smirking. Without thinking I launch towards him. I feel the ground start to shake as the soldiers fall to the floor. Just as I was about to reach him I feel a blast shoot me in the back. I lay right next to his feet staring up at him.

"Joy!" Both my sisters call out to me. I try to get up but kept falling. He was right by me and I can't even get to him as I start to feel myself lose consciousness.

I groan triedly flipping on my back crying. I see the soldiers grab the girls and Luke while they are trying to reach out to me. Octavia starts to throw icicles at the soldiers, and one of them fell as it landed right in his chest. The soldiers instantly put the handcuffs around my sisters and Lily. I see them wiggle struggling to get out of their grips. I look back to see that they pull my dad out the car carrying him before they put him on a stretcher to a helicopter.

"No!" I groan out in pain. I gain enough strength to reach my arm out trying to stop them, but Dr. Whittaker kicks me in the face. I start to see black spots surround me while Dr. Whittaker bends down looking at my with mischief in his eyes.

"I'm about to have my fun with you." He says laughing as I black out......

# Captured

I slowly open up my eyes to a bright room. My head is pounding crazy and my mouth feels dry. I try to sit up but wince once I feel the pain my body is in, so I gently place my self up blinking getting used to the light. I look around the white room and see multiple doctors moving around paying zero attention to me. I look down at my body and notice that I am in a white set that is a mini shirt and shorts. My chest seem to have white sticky tabs and other wires attached. I go to speak out but stop when I feel how dry my throat is. I went to go touch my throat but stop when I feel a collar on it. I try pulling on it hoping my powers will work, but it won't budge. I hear a door open and turn my attention to it as I see Dr. Whittaker walk in with Lindsey behind. My body instantly panics and I fall back out of the seat that I was in and onto the floor.

With tools flying around hitting the floor harshly, I push myself into corner by a desk. The attention is now on me as every doctor looks at me questionably. I start to hyperventilate as see him walking closer. I stare up at him in horror as he bends his knees down to my level.

"Joy, come with me." He says reaching his hand out to me. I push his hand back standing up as I feel my head slightly spinning.

"No, fuck you!" I spit as I move to the other side of the room watching his every step. My mind then drifts back to the events that had happen before and I instantly think of everyone.

"Where is my family? Where is Logan and Megan?!" I say looking frantically across the room like they are going to pop up.

"I killed them all, or maybe they all escaped and left you, or maybe they are all separated thousands of miles away. I will tell you once you come with me." He says smiling. being amused by my reaction.

"I don't believe you, tell me where they are." I say breathing heavily on the brink of passing out again.

He looks at me annoyed as he turns around walking slowly out the room before he speaks to the rest of the doctors. "Put her under rest. I'll come when she wants to listen."

I see the doctors walk towards me with a needle. "No, stay away from me!" I start to scream and the room starts to violently shake. The collar that was on my neck is now next to my feet. The doctors start to hold on to whatever they can as I feel blood leaking out my nose. I look at the door Dr. Whittaker and Lindsey walked out of before I run out sprinting down the hall. I can barely see as I'm passing by multiple doctors in a blur. I see a sign above that says exit and I run faster, but before I can even reach it I feel myself being pulled back. I struggle against the person trying to teleport behind them, but the needle is being stuck inside my neck. I feel my body going limp as I'm being dragged to a room.

I'm trying to keep my eyes open as long as I possibly can but whatever was in the needle is pulling me towards darkness. I feel as the guard who was carrying me toss me onto the floor of a room. I weakly try to pull me body up, but keep falling. I give up and accept my fate as I shut my eyes laying hopelessly.-

I woke up again and this time I'm in a different room. I still have all these wires wrapped around me and the small outfit I had on. I stand up and look around the room just to realize it's not even a room I'm standing in, it's a cell. Outside the cell is a dark green room that has nothing but a desk and filing cabinets on the side. Inside the cell the entire thing is clear glass with holes which are probably for me to breath. The cell seems to be the only thing making the room light as it had a bright lightbulb hanging inside, while the room outside doesnt have any. I turn around seeing that every furniture piece inside, like the bed, desk and toilet is all grey.

Too tired to even scream I sit down on the bed before I hear a tap on the glass. I turn to my right startled by the sound, but even more startled to find Liberty? What is she possibly doing here? Liberty looks at me and smiles lightly. Yeah I must be imagining things again. I shake my head turning the other way until she calls my name.

"Joy." I don't believe it's her and continue to face the opposite way that also had another cell attached to mine, but it had barely any light. I then realize that I'm in the middle of the other 2 cells in the room.

"Joy!" She said again and this time without thinking I turn my head to her, but when I turn my head to her I see an electricity shock from the ceiling shoot her through her back. She groans hissing at the pain.

"Sorry, assholes I'm still learning how to control it." She says still staring up at a corner that has a camera. I look at her confused.

"Are you real?"

"Wow, I would assume after having classes with you since freshman year that you would know I'm real." She says sitting up slowly on her knees. If this were before I meant Logan I would be ecstatic that my lifelong crush is actually talking to me, and that she is actually acknowledging me. But because of this lucky situation I'm in it's not the victory I was expecting.

"Sorry, been through a lot. Thought my mind was playing tricks." I say scooting closer to where she is at, also sitting on my knees.

"Yeah that's understandable."

An awkward silence comes over us for a few minutes before I've decided I couldn't take it.

"So what was that thing that just shocked you." I ask curious to what happened.

"Well when I, or anyone I guess, uses their powers this cage thing detects it and shocks us." She explains. I look down to her neck to see if she has the collar I had on and realize that she doesn't. I touch my neck and feel that it has not been placed back on.

"What are your powers?"

"I can control people when I speak. I just tell them something and they do it. But I didn't mean to control you, I just wanted your attention and it happened accidently." She says twidling her thumbs.

"Its fine besides I think we kind of have the same powers, I can control people, but I just think about what I want them to do instead. And I have a few others" I reply back. She goes to speak again but we hear a deep voice on the other side of me.

"Can you guys, I don't know, shut the fuck up." I squint my eyes over there as I try to see who is in the cage next to us because for some odd reason there is no light in his. I look at Liberty who is doing the same as I am.

"Who are you-" She goes to speak but another shock shoots her in the back even harder this time. She yelps as she lays on the floor trying to soothe her back. This time she starts shaking and passed out.

"Liberty!" I call out as the person next to us laughs out loud.

"Nevermind keep talking, that was funny as fuck."

I look over at him stepping away from Liberty. I go by his cage putting my whole entire face on it squinting even more, but he pops his face out of no where making me jump back startled. I hear his laugh again as he stays in the light this time eyeing me. I put my hand over my chest to calm myself down while looking over him. I know this guy.

"Ryan?" I ask getting closer to him no longer scared. He looks at me confused until he realizes who I am.

"Well ,well, well, if it ain't Joy." He say smirking. I glare sharply at him as he used to bully me Megan when we were in middle school. He was really an ass and apparently still is one.

"Ryan what the hell? What are you doing here?" I say as realizing having my ex- crush and ex- bully to the sides of me. Although I wouldn't call Ryan an ex- bully as he still would bother me and Megan time to time in highschool.

"Well what do you think you're doing here dumbass? You're getting tortured, that's what." He answers sarcastically. I glare at him again before turning back to Liberty and seeing if she's okay, but she's still knocked on the floor.

"Hey Dr. Creepy come help, she passed out." I turn to the camera that's on the wall and yell out hoping someone is atleast listening. I look back once I hear Ryan laughing again.

"What the hell are you laughing at this time?" I ask getting irritated with him.

"They don't give a fuck about you, you know that right?"

"Oh and they totally give a fuck about you, right?"

"Well I would assume so as I am the son of Dr. Creepy." He says leaning back on one of the walls of the cage. Ryan? The son of Dr. Whittaker? No way. I then start to think back when I heard his last name, Whittaker. Ryan Whittaker is Dr. Whittaker's son. That honestly could explain plenty of things about Ryan. I stare at him tilting my head.

"Well if he cares about you why are you in a cell like the rest of us?" I ask genuinely confused. All of a sudden like a switch he turns his head glaring at me.

"My father cares about me. Don't go putting stupid ideas in your head, Joy. I'm in here to be observed, I will be out soon." He says going back to his dark corner. Okay talk about daddy issues.

I shake my head, not really caring about his little fit. I go to scream at the camera again before I see the door open. Dr. Whittaker walks in taking slow steps with his hands behind his back.

"Hello Joy."

I roll my eyes at him "Are you going to actually help or just stand there?"

"I will help your friend, if you come with me willingly and don't try anything."

I look at him questionably taking in his words. "What will you do to me?"

"Nothing that would kill you." He replies playfully.

"You're going to hurt me." I state.

"Well I thought that was a given. I just need to analyze and run some test on you. If you do your part it shouldn't hurt too bad." He replied

No matter what situation I'm still going to get hurt. If I'm going to be in pain I might as well help someone else not be. "Okay, help her first." I say giving in.

"That's my girl." He says stroking his beard. I visibly cringe as he speaks again. "Guards come in and take Liberty to the health center." The guards come in opening the cell with a combination pin that's on the outside. Dr. Whittaker comes in with a collar quickly rushing to me.

"That last collar wasn't strong enough for your powers I underestimated you." He says snapping it on my neck. I flinch as I feel a small sting where he closed it at. Before we fully leave the room he looks at the cell to my left.

"I'll check on you later son." He says looking back at Ryan's cage and there is no answer as we walk out the room. While walking down the hallways I see that the whole building is futuristic and white and when we were passing through the hallways some rooms have keypads, some with locks, and some have none. When looking outside the rooms, they had a big window next to them where you can see them testing on others.

When I was passing by one room there was a little Asian boy who looked scared out his mind while the doctors walked towards him with a drill. I stopped infront of it instantly and Dr. Whittaker watched with me.

"Ah yes, the drill process. It's for certain indiviuals whose powers are dormant. As they drill into the brain their bodies release the dormant powers because they are under too much stress. We make sure that they don't drill too far to kill the subject. It's also a great tool for everyone as we can see how strong their powers are when their brain is being attacked." He says looking amazed at the boy who is now screaming. The boy is rapidly turning into multiple people at once while the doctors keep drilling into his head.

"See, now we know that boy is a shapeshifter and we can train him according to that power." He says pointing.

"He's just a little boy though." I whisper mindlessly, while tears begin to fill my eyes.

"He is, and when we're done with him he's going to be great." He says putting his hands on my shoulder turning me the other direction. I reluctantly look away as we keep walking into a room where multiple doctors are scrambling around. It looks sort of like the rooms we just passed.

"Sit up on that chair right there." Dr. Whittaker say pointing to the chair that has arm and leg restraints. I start to back up scared about what is going to happen next. I feel Dr. Whittaker's arm push me forward. I try to push his arm off of me put it won't budge. "Don't even try it Joy." He says finally sitting me in the chair.

A few of the doctors come and wrap the arm and leg restraints around me deathly tight. I start to panic and move trying to get out the chair.

"Remember what I said, if you do your part it won't hurt as much. So stop resisting."

I shake my head ignoring him until I feel a slap come across my face. I stop moving instantly glaring at him. He grabs my chin harshly, squeezing it.

"Stop resisting Joy. That slap was unecessary if you would've listened I wouldn't have to do that." He said letting go of my chin. I feel the tear run down my face as he turns his back at me putting on gloves and other things.

"So far we know the abilities you possess. We just don't know how far we can take them yet. You have strong powers, stronger than a lot others and you can do much more if we push you little by little. You have super strength, telekinesis, teleportaion, and I do believe you have some hyper- awareness and a bit of telepathy. Not strong enough to read people's minds, but enough to hear thoughts from others. You also seem to get into people's heads to control their bodies, but not minds. So because your other sense are so heightened we have to do the same for your telepathy and some hyper- awareness." He finishes as he walks across the room gathering more equipment.

"How do you know all that?" I ask shakily.

"I don't know if you have noticed Joy, but I have abilities like you." He stops walking and stands infront of me. I think back to when we were in the basement and Dr. Whittaker was talking about when he said that he got into Megan's mind. Can he possibly be a mind reader too?

"So what are your powers?" I say trying to get some information.

"Abilities, you are not some kind of superhero. Abilities not powers."

I mentally roll my eyes before continuing. "So... what are they?"

"Let's just say I'm connected to all those with abilities." He says before turning back around. How can he be connected to all of us? Did he take some kind of ultimate cure and suddenly become God of those with powers? I need to figure out more if I'm going to be able to leave this place.

"Did you take the cure as well knowing what it was going to do?" I ask on more. He looks at me sharply.

"Enough questions. Don't move and this should be fine." The other doctors grab my face forcing me to stop moving. One of the doctors spreads my eyelids open so that I can't shut them. I instantly start to scream when Dr. Whittaker comes over with a needle. I pull at my restraints harder hoping he isn't going to do what I think he is.

"I just need to stick this fluid into your eye, so that hopefully it will signal the cells in your brain to connect with other's cells." He says coming closer to me. I shake violently as he grabs my face harshly again.

"Would you rather I stick the drill into your head Joy? I promise either one works for me, although it would be a shame to mess that pretty face."

I sit there not saying anything and he squeezes my face more. I slowly shake my head no.

"Exactly what I thought. Now sit still and it'll be over soon." He says as he lets go of my face. My eye that is now burning from not blinking is dangerously close to the needle. I feel as Dr. Whittaker inserts it into my eye and I can feel the liquid stream through my eye into the back of my head. It felt like nothing until I start to feel burning sensation course through my head. The doctors let go of me as I start to scream even louder. I go to try and put my hands to my head, but the restraints don't allow me. I shut my eyes as the pain increases through my head hitting every nerve.

I lay on the side of my face as sweat drips down my neck. The burning stops painfully slow and I lean back in the seat shaking softly. Dr. Whittaker takes my collar off with a small controller that he took out his front pocket. The doctors surrounding us gasp as he does this and go by the emergency button on the side of the room. He grabs my face as I lay still not having enough energy to even try using my powers. Dr. Whittaker stands there staring at me.

"Did you hear my thoughts that I'm sending to you Joy?" I didn't hear a damn thing he thought. Once he realizes I'm not giving him an answer he walks over to me. He opens my nearly shut eye and analyzes it. He takes a quick look at it and seems dissapointed as he pushes my head back.

"Dammit! All your eye did was turn fucking purple." He yells hitting a nearby table. Did I hear that correctly? He looks at the doctors huddled in the corner of the room. "One of you idiots come over here and get her a mirror. She's too weak to even attempt to use her powers." None of the doctors move as they look at me waiting for me to attack any moment. Dr. Whittaker groans and clips the collar back on me. Everyone then moves over to where I am at warily while one hands my a mirror. I couldn't lift my arms to grab it so they turn my face toward the mirror and open my eye. And just like Dr. Whittaker said, it's a very faint dark purple. I sob again as I see this change to my body. What will be next, my hair, my body, my face? I don't want to be a lab rat that they can poke and prob on every day for the rest of my life. I need to leave.

"Maybe she's just too weak to feel something right now, we will check on her in a few hours when she has some rest. Two of you go take her back to her cage and here, take off the collar once she has been placed in it." He tries to say calmly, while handing them the controller. Two men come and lift me up as we make it back to the room where my cell is. I see that they start typing a pin and I open my eyes a little hoping that they wouldn't see me. I get a few of the digits, but one of the doctors look at me.

"Is she awake?" The one putting in the pin asks.

"I don't think so she seems too weak." The one holding me says.

"Well if she wakes up and tries to leave I'm blaming you." He laughs as he finishes the rest of the code. They open my cell and toss me on the bed taking off my collar. I roll over to see if Liberty is in here, but her cell is empty, so I roll back over in a fetal position.

5 7 2 1 those are the numbers I saw before they looked at me. 5 7 2 1 are the numbers I will remember when I destroy this place.

# My Joy

**Logan's POV**

I have to leave. I'm sitting in this glass cage damn near losing my mind as Dr. Whittaker is talking about how I'm his prized possession and I'm a valuable asset to his "plan". I need to get to my siblings, I need to get to Joy. My heart pains as I start to think about how I failed all of them. I was supposed to protect them but instead I got myself captured in the hands of a madman.

I woke up earlier to him knocking on the cage smiling brightly. The first thing he did once he saw my eyes open was to start talking endlessly. Not to mention my head is spinning in circles and my body is too sore to even tell him to shut up.

"Oh Logan, you're going to be better, bigger, and greater. You're my idea, the idea." He says staring at me in complete awe. He turns around while he pulls a stool up the front of my cage.

"So how do you feel?"

I stare at him in disbelief. How do I feel? I feel like if I wasn't in so much pain, I would have already turned and torn his head off his shoulders.

"Let me out and I'll show you." I spit out. He laughs and clasps his hands together.

"C'mon now Logan! I'm just trying to converse."

"Converse? You call trapping me in a cage away from the people I love most, conversing?" I say gathering more energy.

"If you would've come willingly I wouldn't have to do all this." He says waving my comment off.

"You fucking played with us like toys! Why the hell would I come willingly, you're batshit crazy." I say finally standing up and banging my hand on the wall infront of me. I start to feel the claws slip through, but they slowly retract as I start to feel more sleepy. I fall back losing all the energy I gathered and lay my head on the wall.

"I see that the blockers are working perfectly. You were about to turn, weren't you? Look above at those blue lights Logan. They stop you from using your powers and turning into that beautiful creature." He says pointing to the top of the cage. I squint my eyes looking at the blue lights and my eyes start to water. I don't know whether it's because those lights are so bright or the fact that I'm away from everyone I could have possibly ever loved. My whole entire life I thought I would be successful, that I would actually be on top. Now I'm an experimental pet for a man who's half crazy. My heart pains just thinking about the normal life I used to have. I start to feel hopeless as tears fall freely. I hear Dr. Whittaker sigh as he sees the tears fall.

"Boy there ain't no reason to cry now. I'm not going to hurt you if that's what you're thinking. Only if you listen we ain't gonna have no problems." He says now standing in front of my cage. He types some pin in before he steps inside closing the door.

"What the hell are you doing?" I ask sitting up more alert.

"Logan, I will tell you everything you want to know in exchange for your cooperation. You are a very important part of my plan and I need you to know that you can trust me." He says sitting on the small bed in the corner.

"Trust you? You're a liar and a manipulator, I am not trusting you for shit." I say glaring at him. He sighs again and rubs his temple.

"That's understandable. What would you need to get me to trust you?" He asks staring at me.

"I want to know your plan. You say you want me to trust you and that you're not going to hurt me, but here I am kidnapped with my friends and family gone." I say breathing heavily.

"It may seem bad now but when we, the Supremes, rule the world, we're going dominate and conquer. We are going to be Alphas, top tier, and no one is going to think about destroying us as we will destroy them first." He says looking as if he's lost in thought about his little fantasy.

"Supremes? Who are the supremes?"

"The supremes are you, us, all the people with the strongest, most dangerous powers are supremes, and you, my Logan, are the best supreme out there. Your abilities are out of this world, you're the only one I have known of and I'm going to keep you." He says with his arms on his knees. I glare at him. Like hell I would stay with him!

"To be exact, you want me and other people with strong powers to conquer the world with you? You're even crazier than I thought." Dr. Whittaker looks at me sharply and his eye slightly twitches.

"I'm not crazy! Crazy would be having people tell you your whole life that you are useless and won't ever get anything you deserve. Underestimating me constantly over and over again, "William you're ignorant." "William you're a madman." "William you're an idiot and won't get anywhere in life!" Well guess what? I single-handedly created special abilities for humans all over the world that none of you would have if I didn't give them to you! Every one of my creations should be kissing my feet but no, all you do is whine and bitch about it. So because you want to whine I'll give you something to whine about!" He says standing up and opening my cage. He leaves it open and walks out of the room. I take this as my chance of freedom, but before I can even think of escaping he calls some guards in and they stand in front of the cage.

"Now Logan, you really pissed me off. I wasn't going to do this, but I think you need a lesson. A lesson proving that I am NOT crazy." He says as his face is red and sweaty. He looks more disappointed than angry at me as he is trying to control his breathing.

"Take him to room 44." He simply says before the guards come and drag me. I try to pull away from them but they won't budge. I grunt and thrash in their arms as they drag me down the long white hallways. We pass some rooms until there is a room that says 44 in big, black letters. The guards toss me in there and I look around the room. The room is just plain grey with a chair in the middle of it. I feel beads of sweat dripping down my face as I anticipate what is next. I hear the door open and I instantly scoot back on the floor. Dr. Whittaker steps in tsk-ing.

"Logan, go sit in the chair." He says rolling up his white sleeves. I noticed as he has a long, large scar along his forearm. It looked as if whoever did it meant for it to be deep as it looks scarred over. While I was staring at his arm I didn't realize that he was in front of me. He reached towards me and I moved swiftly across the floor.

"Don't make this harder than it has to be Logan. Get in the chair." I shake my head.

"Fine have it your way." He pulls out a small remote control and suddenly the light in the room turns a glowy, dark blue and my head spins rapidly. I start to see a blurred figure come in front of me and roughly sit me in the chair. He puts the straps on me and I hear him grunting and mumbling nonsense. He keeps mumbling louder until he starts to yell. "Shut up! Shut up now! I'm tired of you telling me what to think. Leave!"

It could've been my imagination, but I believe he was yelling at himself. He shakes his head smiling.

"Do you think this is funny? I'll show you funny." He says staring at the ceiling. I blankly stare at him as my head was now spinning painfully. He darts his eyes at me, looking as if he didn't realize I was listening. His eyes go twitching before he bangs his hands on his head abruptly.

"Fuck!" He says marching out of the room and leaving me alone. I listen outside the door as I hear grunting and objects clattering on the floor, then it goes quiet.

I sit anticipating what was going to happen next, but nothing ever did. At first I was relieved, until I kept sitting and sitting and sitting, as the hours ticked away. Nothing happened. Not outside the door not around me, nowhere.

It felt like a couple of days have passed as my body feels restless and I have to use the restroom, but as I screamed nothing happened.

My bladder was released multiple times as I continued to sit in the chair and wait. I wanted to eat, something to drink, even fucking garbage sounded delicious. I could feel the air around me, every molecule drifting pass me as the sweat dripped onto my shirt. I couldn't even sleep and felt as if the whole world stopped while I sat, and sat and sat into the chair.

I gave up a while ago trying to scream as no one came to help anyways. As my head lays low I feel the atmosphere around me change as the door opened. I jolt my head up thankful for whoever it was, but as the figure came in I saw Dr. Whittaker.

I stared at him until I put my head down, weeping again.

"Don't cry Logan I'll let you go. Only if you agree to my terms." He said patting my head.

I glance up at him hopefully as my heart starts to fill with joy. I go to say yes but remembered my predicament. I can't give up that easily.

I can't succumb to him because I don't won't feel this pain, I have to endure it. Not just for Luke, Lily, or Joy, but for me. I want to leave but my future out there is worse than in here.

"No." I choke out.

"No?" He says removing his hand from my head.

"No." I repeat again.

"Boy, you are something else. Enjoy the next week by yourself." He says laughing turning out of the room, this time he clicks a button as the blue light shines brighter. My body instantly shakes as the shivers jump up my back.

The pain worsens and I sit. I continue to sit as the light pierces into my skin. As my body excretes any liquid inside me. As my stomach eats itself alive and I stare into pure nothingness.

I feel myself crying as I have been doing these past days. I cry until I felt a warm embrace surround me. I look to the side of me and see Joy.

"Oh, Logan. Look at yourself." She says rubbing my cheek softly.

"Joy?" I asked knowing that this is probably a figment of my imagination. Nonetheless, I was glad to see her.

"Logan you have to leave." She said looking at me like a precious diamond.

"Joy, I have to stay here, I have to be strong. I can't give myself to him. I need to be there for you guys when I leave" I say leaning into her. She grabs my head as she pushes me into her chest.

"You can't get to us if there is nothing left of you Logan. I know you want to be strong, but I need you alive." She said rubbing my head softly. I start crying again as I look up into her eyes.

"I won't leave you Joy, I love you." I say as she wipes my tear away.

"I know you won't. Don't let him get to you Logan, I love you." She says kissing my cheek as she fades away.

"Joy?! Come back to me please!" I say shaking my head in confusion. I want to be strong I really do, but I think it's time for me to give up. I start yelling as I feel myself fall apart.

"Dr. Whittaker! I give up." I yell praying he hears me. I continue to yell his name over and over until I hear the door open.

"So you finally caved in." He says smirking.

"Just get me out of here." I say panting slowly.

"Whatever you want." He says as he unclips my straps......

I totally said I was going to post 2 weeks ago and totally lied. Sorry!!

# F*ck This Lab

## Third person POV

## 2 MONTHS EARLIER

Dr. Whittaker stands outside the lab cursing lowly as he thinks of his stupid experiments that aren't progressing at all. He has tried over and over to make his very own creations to call his, but none seem to want to be. He holds onto the rail outside the lab building while staring at the sun rising.

He's been here all night again and still failed. Failing is something he also seemed to keep doing. He wants to stop failing so that he can prove a point, not just to himself but everyone. He continues to stare at the rising sun as he hears the door behind him open.

"Dr. Whittaker, would you mind if I go home now? I've been here the whole night and would like to spend some time with my family." Lindsey's light British accent spoke softly as she stood by the door looking afraid.

He tilts his head a little to glance at her. "Of course you want to quit. You're fucking useless. "

Lindsey gasps a bit and bites her lip. "Sorry, you're right. I don't know what I was thinking." She's says laughing nervously. She goes to shut the door but Dr. Whittaker stops her.

"Have a damn backbone. You can go home, we have nothing left to achieve anyways." He mumbles while completely turning to her and stroking his beard. Lindsey looks a little reluctant to leave until Dr. Whittaker raised his eyebrows at her expectedly and she rushes off.

"Damn nutjob." He murmurs under his breath sighing. He waits until he can see Lindsey's car drive off from the lab and returns back in. He looks at the garbage full of dead rats that weren't strong enough to withhold true power (as Dr. Whittaker liked to call it). All of them could've have strong domineering abilities if they weren't such animals.

He kicks the trash full of rats grunting slightly. The rats fall without so much as a breath onto the floor. He stares for almost 10 minutes hoping something would happen. He was damn near desperate as he watched the stale, cold rats lay emotionless. He felt a tear slip down his face as he slowly walks out of the room, turning off the lab's light never looking away from the trash can once until he fully shuts the door, walked down the stairs, and into his car driving away with despair.

One thing he didn't know was that one of the rats popped up as soon as he left. The rat looked around the room and quickly hopped into a small hole in the side of the wall. The rat walks with its small feet through a short tunnel and to the outside. Shaking off all the lint and dirt the little rat walks its infectious body across the street contaminating and killing everything in between. -2 weeks later

He couldn't believe the news, he was almost in disbelief. Dr. Whittaker has actually created a disease, his own disease. The world is in a frenzy as deaths rise and hope seems to decline. But Dr. Whittaker was excited, this was the opportunity. He had a whole world full of people that he can inject his little serum with. Trial and error will occur, but nonetheless the errors will be part of the bigger picture.

He eagerly walked into the lab with all his coworkers staring at him hopefully. He knows they are probably looking at him with the hope of curing this disease and not the hope that he has for this planet. Unfortunately, they simply don't understand.

"Ahhh my lovely workers, today is a new day! My experiments did not go in vain, they were not wasted. I know you truly believe I'm crazy, a madman perhaps, but I just handed out an opportunity for the people of Earth; for us." He says with the biggest smirk on his face. One of the workers had an expression of grief on her face as she walks up to Dr. Whittaker with a stiff walk and glares up at him.

"An opportunity you say?" She asks rhetorically.

"Yes, I do believe so."

"Tell that to my dead husband." She said not once breaking eye contact. His face turns grim as he looks at her sorrowful expression.

"It's not my fault he was weak. If he were strong, he could've made it to the next step of our plan." He responds promptly. The young doctor has unshed tears in her eyes as she glares at him one more moment before storming out.

"Now, is there anybody else in here who is worried about the wrong things? We need to focus on the present, the thing that matters most. We have a new world to create and if you want your emotions to get the best of you then you might as well leave now." He says staring at the group of white coats.

Most of them leave as they want no part of Dr. Whittaker's plan. The ones that did stay were there because of fear. The fear of what would happen if Dr. Whittaker did rule the world and they needed a place in it, so they stayed. They stayed through it all; all of the failed serums, all of Dr. Whittakers tantrums, and all the dead bodies that followed along the way.

Until one day the workers come in to see Dr. Whittaker excitedly packing little cases of vials into a small suitcase. He turns around at the noise and clasps his hands. "We have finally done it! My vaccine is working to perfection and the new age of humans shall begin." Everone in the room looks at him skeptical.

"Well what are you waiting for? Start helping me pack these vials. The government wants us to send these our as soon as possible." He says turning back to packing. The workers reluctantly but surely started packing the vials one by one.

Dr. Whittaker keeps packing as Lindsey comes up behind him and taps his shoulder lightly. "Dr. Whittaker?" She asks softly. He turns around to look at her with a grin. "What is it Lindsey?"

"What exactly did we accomplish? I mean I know everyone is going to have true power but what even is true power? I mean how are we even going to control it?" She asks spilling her concerns.

"My Lindsey, my most loyal worker from the start, keep putting your faith in me like you have from the very start and you will see the truth." He says placing both of his hands on the sides of her face. Lindsey shakes her head as a result of not knowing what to do. He let's go of her face as he clears his throat. Everyone stares up at him waiting.

"Today is the day. My vaccine will be placed all across the world for everyone to have. Now do not be fooled, there will be plenty of more deaths, there will be plenty of more pain, but there will be special people along the way who are already in the making of my true power. We will be attending some facilities and schools to make sure that this is evenly distributed and gather the most strongest for our new world. Thank you all so deeply for helping, you will be rewarded generously and shall join me in my new world. Now lets gather our supplies and start what I've been dreaming of since I was a kid." He says looking prideful amongst the worker.

The workers though were looking the exact opposite as the fear they had became much worse. They grab all the small vials and start loading them into vans. Dr. Whittaker gives instructions on who and what is going where as he and Lindsey gather into small van together.

"Aren't you ready Lindsey?" He asks her passionately.

Lindsey looks up slowly. "More than ever Whittaker." She stops for a moment before she speaks again. "Where are we going?"

"We are going to a place where I sense the greatest power. I can feel a couple of them in Carson City, Nevada, so we shall go there." Lindsey nods her head before Dr. Whittaker speaks again.

"When I was young the only thing I could dream about was making the world a better place. My father made sure to stop me, but that would've never worked. He tortured me, out of love though to help my mother, but he sure as hell did torture me. The love I had for this world still stayed, but the idea of how to accomplish it changed. You see no one is going to listen when the world is turning into an oven, or when the oceans are polluted, or even if everyone is dying and they know they can fix it. People need real change, a change that is going to make them listen and I am ready to be that change. My father would've told me 'William such silly dreams is what made your mother sick' but I'm not little William anymore. And my mother, she would've lived if my father only listened to her 'silly dreams'. I can't truly blame my father though as he did make me the man I am today, my mother not so much. Either way I'm here today and because of him I now know what the world needs." Dr Whittaker finishes looking out the window. Lindsey stares at him confused as she slowly turned her head to the window waiting for their destination......

# Escaped

Logans POV

Test, after test, after test and I'm still here. Stuck, trapped I'm my own mind and no where to get out. I've lost all track of time and I don't even know if my family is alive, or even if Joy was still alive.

I look at the transparent walls of my cage waiting to see if they were coming to take me yet. They're late today, and they've never been late before.

We have a routine, and that routine consists of me going into the blue room as soon as I wake up and get tortured for hours on end, or as Dr. Whittaker says enduring pain to withstand "true power". Then I would eat breakfast. I used to eat breakfast before I went into the blue room, but I would throw up everything, which made Dr.

Whittaker make me eat afterwards. Because breakfast is all they will give me some days, its loaded with random brown mush that I'm forced to eat, and if I don't they will take me back to the blue room while they torture me some more.

Then I would go with the whitecoats so that they can test how strong I got from earlier that day, while injecting serums every now and then to help my newfound abilities. And finally I would go back to my cage and wait hours for dinner to arrive, if they even wanted me eat.

I'm supposed to be checked for my powers now with the whitecoats, but apparently something happened in the blue room that I can't seem to remember as I blacked out. The last thing I heard was the whitecoats arguing with Dr. Whittaker spewing facts about how I wasn't supposed to transform, or how I was becoming something they couldn't handle. It seemed serious as none of them ever talk back to Whittaker. I didn't hear much before I blacked out completely and made it back here where I'm waiting continuos hours on end wondering if they would even come to get me.

Sometimes to make the time go fast I think of the outside world and how its like. I wonder if there ever was a true vaccine and if people are back to normal, or how maybe my parents are still looking for me and my siblings, that's if they're even still alive. Nonetheless, I like to think of numerous things whether they are good or bad, because anything is better than sitting around all day, every day wondering if I'm going to make it out.

No knowledge of time, no reassurance from anyone, and most of all no hope. When Dr. Whittaker left me in room 44 I had a belief that this would be temporary, that in some way I would be saved along with those I've loved, but for quite some time I've been thinking otherwise.

Times like these I wonder if the government even still exists, if morals or any type of humanity would change my current situation, but I know better. I known better for a while that this may be the rest of my life.

I continue to sit on the ground of my cage waiting till I hear anything, even as small as a mouse lightly walking in the vents, until I finally hear voices outside the room. They don't know yet, but I'm not supposed to be able to hear outside of my cage. A few months back, or atleast it felt like, I left the blue room and got tested for any new abilities. Nothing happened until I went back to my room and started to hear the doctors outside the room talk about how disappointing it is that I haven't had any new abilities in a while. Usually my collar would shock me or the light receptors in the room would notify Dr. Whittaker that one of my powers were in use, but nothing happened. I tried to hear farther then right outside my door but it wouldn't work.

Regardless, I used this new ability to hear what the whitecoats would say as I'm testing my powers and try to get insight on anything useful that could help me escape. So far nothing, but that doesn't mean that there isn't something I can't find.

I turn my attention back to the door and it turns out I'm hearing Dr. Whittaker and Lindsey whispering aggressively to each other.

"Lindsey if I hear one more word come out your mouth about Logan I will lose it!"

"Whittaker I don't think you understand, he's becoming too strong. We have limited options here and we need to come up with the fastest one now." She says in a soft voice.

I hear Dr. Whittaker groan and tap his feet impatiently. "You mean to tell me that he is getting to strong to the point where my mechanisms don't work on him anymore?"

"Well, your mechanisms are becoming weaker everyday, and once he realizes that we are all screwed. The only thing really keeping him in his human form is his fear. He can transform at any given moment if he feels as if he can overpower us. We need to make sure that he doesn't realize it. And that also means no more torturing him until he can't think straight, that's how he transformed today."

I raised my eyebrows in shock of this new info. I can turn. I can turn right now and leave. I can leave and never see Dr. Whittakers face ever again. I stand up in my cage anticipating their next move.

"I thought fear is what stops him from turning, why can't I keep 'torturing' him to keep him in check?" He says as I hear his hand stroke his crunchy beard.

"His fight or flight kicks in as his natural instinct is to protect himself, so he turns under distress. You need to do more mental torture and not physical or otherwise we can't stop him like today."

He grunts in frustration typing in my pass code to my door. He steps inside the room with Lindsey behind him and stares at me as I am standing up staring back as well.

"Why are you standing up, boy? Ain't you supposed to be burnt out from all that stress you had today." He says walking carefully up to my cage. I continue to stare and a small grin starts to form.

I know something that he doesn't. I will get out of here today, I will find my family, I will find Joy, and I will kill this son of a bitch alongside every whitecoat in this building. Lindsey's information made me feel less afraid as I now know the truth. Dr. Whittaker laughs at my expression as he opens my cage and grabs my shoulder roughly throwing me onto the floor. Lindsey gives Whittaker a warning glare and picks me off the floor gently.

"Come now, Logan. You aren't going to test with us today, Dr. Whittaker is going to take you to the blue room again to do some mental exercises." She says leading me out the room with Dr. Whittaker behind us. They haven't had a clue on what's going to happen.

"Oh, is he really or do you mean he's going to continue torturing me." I say sarcastically. She shakes her head still walking to the blue room. I stop in my tracks and look at Dr. Whittaker. "Are you going to 'mentally train' me or torture me?" I ask tilting my head. Dr. Whittaker keeps a stoic expression and clasps his hands in front of him.

"You got lot of nerve talking to me like that. And I've told you time again that you are enduring true power not torture. Now if you know what's best for you, you will walk down this hall and get your ass into that room with a damn smile on your face." I hear Lindsey stop walking noticing that we are still stopped and she slowly walks over to us.

"No, if you know what's best for you, I suggest you run." I say grabbing my collar full strength and throwing it to the floor. It breaks into small pieces shattering on the ground as I hear Lindsey gasps. I start to feel immense power course through me as my nerves run through me. This is it. I did it, I finally did it.

I start to transform as I hear the squishy noises of my talons lengthing. I fall to my knees as sharp blades pierce through the back of my skin causing blood to drip down. My back contorts into different shapes as my hair sheds off and my skin turns black with a blue undertone. My teeth pop out as new thin sharp ones form underneath. My limbs feel almost reptilian as I stand from the floor at almost 8 ft of glory. I yell an animalistic growl as I see the white halls are now red and the blaring alarm rings annoyingly. I look around to find Dr. Whittaker and Lindsey gone in a crowd of people running. I see some of the patients fighting against the whitecoats and some of them struggling to take off their collars.

The guards come running in shooting the patients with the blue bullets I run towards them as they try to shoot me down but struggled as I raise my hand and sliced all their necks with ease. I snarl running down the hallways killing as many whitecoats and guards as possible. I help rip off some of the patients collars as they use their powers to fight back. The whitecoats, obviously losing the fight scream in agony as their own karma reflects back on them.

I ripped the throat out on some random doctor as I see the once blaring red lights turn blue. I was worried until I realized that the light wasn't effecting me at all. I can't say that for others as the patients fall to the ground in agony. I grunt impatiently as I look for a way to turn it off. I look in the hallways and find Lindsey in one of the rooms that was strictly meant for doctors and it seemed to be the control room. The door is wide open as she has her hand on a lever breathing heavily. She puts her hands on her chest trying to calm her self down as she probably thinks she's safe now. But the minute she sees me looking at her she starts hyperventilating.

I stalk into the room bending my head to be able to get into the room, and menacingly walk towards her. She lets go of the lever as she reaches into her pocket and pulls out a syringe. She struggles to keep it in her hand as I get closer. I reach her finally and back her into a wall. She starts crying as her hand can't keep the syringe straight. I grab it from her crushing it in my hand. I drop the remaining syringe on the floor as she looks down at the crushed pieces in despair. I blow air out of my nose as it touches her hair blowing it out the way. I laugh but it came out more like an animal growling and Lindsey loses it as urine falls down her leg.

I laugh even more at that as I start to speak in a gruff, harsh voice. "Turn off the blue light." She shakily turns her head back to the lever and reaches it. The lights go back to red and I hear more commotion outside. "Is there a way to make every patient's collar come off?"

She tries to speak as she sputters spit every where, scared to even think straightly. I bang my hand right above her head as the wall crumbles a bit on to her hair. She jumps again as snot leaks from her nose. She moves her head to the other side of the room pointing towards the controls where the cameras are at. I grab her arm moving her to work it.

"Turn them off, now." Of course she shakily moves her hand to a red button and I look at the cameras to see all of the collars falling off people. "Now open up all the cages." I say roughly. She looks at me in a pleadful way. I raise my hand and slice her cheek open as blood gushes out. She screams as her hand reaches to hold on to it. I dig my nails into her shoulder glaring at her. "Open the fucking cages now!" I demand and without hesitation this time she presses a button releasing the patients.

She stares down at the floor as I can hear her tears streaming. I lift her face up roughly so she can stare at me. "Where is Dr. Whittaker? And dont fucking stutter."

To no avail she stutters tremendously. "He's eit- either on a helicopter, go- gone, or just dead." I snarl digging my hand more into her face. She screams more and I get more aggravated. "Shut the fuck up! Where is my family and Joy's? And do not lie to me as I will rip your head from you body." I say having no more patience.

"I don't kno- know where your sister is at, or Joy's and Joy he- herself," I growl at that and she rushes to get her next words out "but your brother and her dad are here." I peak my head up at that.

"Luke and Howard are here? Where!?" She points to the camera and I see Luke and Howard, who still seems to be in a coma, behind some guards who have them at gun point. I grunt at the guns being held towards them. I look at the bottom of the camera to see what room they are in. Then I turn back at Lindsey who is still shaking as she knows what's about to happen. "I would say thank you, but you don't deserve it." I say pulling her closer to me.

"B- bu- but-" and before she could even finish I rip her arm from her body biting into it like a piece of chicken. I throw the remaining arm back and I reach at her neck and throw her full forces against the cameras. The cameras smash as they start to glitch and the wires began popping out. I then pick her up by her leg and toss her outside the room. All yelling and body movement seize from her as she lays on the ground eyes wide in terror.

I don't pay any mind to the people screaming as they saw Lindsey's body being thrown out of the room, as I rushed to room 124 where I saw my brother and Joy's dad. I rip open the door and see the room that looked like a big arena had a bridge that went halfway and it opened up into a big circle you could stand on. I look up to see the guards in shock and my brother as he looked up at me. He seemed to be scared as he has barely seen my monster form before, but he still appeared slightly relieved.

"Logan?" He asked lightly. I stare and nod my head to let him know it is me. The guards look at our small interaction and start shooting. When they realize nothing is slowing me down, they start pleading hysterically. I start slicing and dicing these fuckers until they are unrecognizable. I reach Logan and Howard as I turn back into my human form.

Luke stares up at me in disbelief before pulling me into a deep hug. I wrap my arms around him with tears threatening to spill. He pulls back before he rests his hands on my shoulder and stare back at me.

"Dude you're naked." He says laughing and patting the side of my face. I roll my eyes and grab onto Howard.

"Yep missed you too. Now c'mon lets go. We don't have to much time." He nods his head while I lift Howard up on my shoulders while slowly transforming back into my monster form. We run down the halls again and find the exit. We see other patients escapung as we run full force until we reach the outside. I look and see that we are hidden by a forest. I turn my head up to the sky and see helicopters surrounding the building. Guards jump from them with guns shooting erratically. The patients go back to fighting as some continue to run in the forest protected by the trees. The guards start shooting at us specifically and I throw spikes directly into their chests as the fall onto the grass.

I think we are safe until I see several helicopters flying above me and Luke. Multiple guard jumps down and stand surrounding us. I roar an animalistic growl as I put Howard down and attack. I grabbed a guard by their helmet crushing their skull as the blood seeps into my hand. I throw the guards body whose head I smashed and tossed it by a group a guards as they flew into a tree because of the force. I stomp over on my hands and feet to a guard trying to shoot at my brother and rip his body in half as his guts spill, tainting the forest floor. The other guards started to run as they saw that act, but I caught up to each of them, ripping their limbs piece by piece.

I look around waiting for another threat, but silence is all I heard. Luke looks up at me in disgust. "Yeah, remind me not to make you mad."

I huff as we continue running. Luke and I kept running until we think we are far enough. We stopped by a lake that sits peacefully contrary to earlier events. Luke drinks the running water, while slurping it like there is no tomorrow. I put Howard down as I turn into my human form once again. I reach the water and rub all the blood off of me. I go back to Howard's limp body and move him slightly as I lay my head on a rock. I grinned happily thinking of my newfound freedom. I stop once I realize the other people I'm missing. Luke looks over after he splashed water on his face.

"Do you think they are alive?" I asked him lightly.

"Who?"

"Everyone." I replied.

"Well hopefully, all we can do is wait and see Logan." He says sitting next to me. We look out by the water as the sun slowly sets. I guess we will just have to wait and seen……

# A year

Joy's POV

"Fuck you!" I hear Liberty scream as a guard tossed her into her cage aggressively.

"Just tell me when and where." The crusty, middle aged guard said as he licked his lips. Liberty scrunches her face into digust as did I, while he walks out the room telling us to sleep tight. I step down from my bed and I lean against yhe wall of my cage onto Liberty's.

"They did a number on you today." I say as I look at the bandage wrapped around her head with blood dripping from it.

She chuckles a bit while tearing a piece of her shirt off her and dabbing it on her forehead. "Yeah, today they wanted me to send everyone in the room a command, without speaking .Those damn 'mental exercises' ain't for the weak."

"We will get out of here. I promise we won't be stuck here getting tortured for Dr. Whittakers use. Just a little longer then we will leave." I say putting my hand up on the glass wall. She puts he hand up and I hear her sniffle as she nods her head slowly.

"I know Joy. I know."

"You can stop trying to give each other false hope. You both know you're not getting out of here." We both turn our heads to Ryan as we both roll our eyes and turn our heads again.

"Ryan just because you have no hope doesn't mean we have to." I say as I close my eyes on the glass.

"I don't need hope, I know my dad is going to get me out of here once I reached my true power."

Me and Liberty both, once again, sigh as we hear him talk about how he is going to get out of here. For some reason he thinks his father will let him out, but we haven't seen Dr. Whittakers face in literal months.

Months ago when the flashing, red lights blared is when Dr. Whittaker disappeared. From what I overheard from the whitecoats, someone from another facility escaped and they needed to put out a siren to all the other facilities just incase there was a rebellion. I remember I was being tortured when the lights went off.

Specifically what I remember, was how much pain I was in that day. They were putting me a pitch black room with others as they made me detect what genders they were, how many people were there, and what powers they had. I couldn't detect so many people at once and so everytime I got something wrong the doctors ordered them to use their powers and hurt me. Then they would bring in a whole new group of people and do the same thing. I'm pretty sure this 'exercise' went on for a whole day as they wouldn't let me go until I got everyone correct. I got burned, cut, stabbed, shot, and much worse.

The only reason I survived is because a couple months before, right around when I first got here, they made me have rapid healing skills.

After hours of torture I never got it correct, I was getting closer, but never correct. As this exercise went on there was one patient wo had strong powers that I could sense, but I had no clue what it was. I told the doctors a guess of what their powers could be, and shocker, I got it wrong. The patient was then demanded to use their powers on me.

And guess what? They had blood bending powers. Lucky me.

The patient obeyed as my blood was starting to boil and I felt myself being burned from the inside out. The blood was curling throughout my body as it leaked out through the holes on my face.

I couldn't handle the pain so I passed out. To tell the truth I was honestly hoping that would be the end of me. I loved the way it felt as I laid flat on the hard floor, even with the rotten smell of my blood. I breathed in slowly waiting till death would grab me and swallow me whole.

Suddenly I heard a faint ringing and a blast of white came in sight. I really thought the gates of Heaven were calling me until I felt a familiar presence. For a quick sec I believed the familiar presence was God, but I found something even more shocking.

It was Megan.

Megan ran over to me and lifted me up. "Liberty? Liberty come on you need to wake up." She said shaking me. I blinked a couple of times before I realized I was actually seeing her. I looked up at her in disbelief as I held onto her tightly. She held on just as tight before she pushed me infront of her grasping onto my hands. "We don't have enough time. I need you to remember Joy."

"Megan is this really you? I missed you- I miss you so much." I say not listening to much of what she's saying. I pull back to hug her again, but she keeps me infront of her.

"Joy I need you to remember, please." She says pleadfully.

I scrunch my eyes in confusion. Why is she speaking in tongues? What exactly am I supposed to be remembering?

"Megan, I'm confused and besides I'm not worried about that. I just can't believe you are really here."

Megan sighs as she looks and me with pity.

"Joy do you remember when I last talked to you?"

I look at her even more confused, the last time we talked she was shot and everyone was running for their lives.

"Megan I don't understand, I'm not understanding- explain what you mean."

"Shit." She cursed lowly. She looks up at me and grips my hand firmly.

"You need to come find us Joy, and remember."

"Us? Who is us, Megan?"

"Your family, Joy. Your sisters and Logan's." She said softly.

I remove my hands from her and put my head down. My family? That is something I truly stopped thinking of a long time ago. I mean don't get it wrong I never forgot about them, but thinking about how I lost every single one of them stopped me from trying to remember them. Remember their laughs, their smiles, their happiness, and their utter pure joy. It hurt too much if I thought of them, the pang in my heart would throb like an aching tooth.

All though they are the main reason I want to leave, I can't think too much as to why or the pain starts back up again.

I feel Megan's stare as she looks surprised that was my reaction to her mentioning my family

I gulped as I looked up at Megan teary eyed "My family? Where are you guys at?"

"We are not where you are. We are at a different facility-" She stops suddenly as she looks behind her. I look behind her to see who's there but I don't see anyone.

"What? Megan, what is wrong?" I ask confused on who is behind her.

"Fuck! Ok Joy I can't say much but he escaped." Megan said as she starts fading away slowly.

"Megan what's going on, who escaped!?"

"He escaped, Logan escaped! We will talk again and I'll tell you where I am. I have to leave now." She says as her faded frame pulls me into a hug. I hug her back as she fully disappears and there is nothing left. I look around in confusion.

"Megan! Mega-" I yell out into nothing until I suddenly hear an alarm blaring. I open my eyes to see the once dark room now red. I shut my eyes quickly as I haven't seen any sort of light in a while. I feel the guards running coming inside the room as they pick me up forcefully and run me outside the room.

Ever since that day, the doctors have been confused on Dr. Whittakers whereabouts and if he's even going to come back. I'm worried about Megan and if I actually saw her or if it was a manifestation of me missing her. But what really got to me was what she said about Logan. Did he really escape? And if he escaped, is he looking for me? I mean I know our relationship is basically non existent as we haven't even talked or seen each other in almost a year. But I love him, I love him a lot and want to see him if I leave.

Although I have a crippling fear of him leaving me with some other super powered chick who he decided to escape with, I do really hope he's perfectly safe and has found his peace, with or without me. In all honesty I can't blame him if he doesn't want me or if he's worried about himself. But if there is a chance that he did escaped, I am happy. I'm happy that he is out and not being tortured. I wouldn't wish this on anyone.

I focus back at the conversation with Liberty who is talking to Ryan. "Ryan your father hasn't been seen in months. For all you know he could be dead."

Ryan bangs his hand and the glass roughly "He is not dead. Watch your mouth when talking about my dad."

"Wow so scared. Go cry about it Ryan." Liberty says putting her hands up sarcastically.

"You know wha-" Ryan goes to say something before the door opens up. We all go quiet as a doctor walks in with a clip board.

"Take her out of the cage." He says pointing at me.

I put my head down without a fight knowing it's not going to do anything. They open the clear door as they snatch me out I see Liberty looking at me with tear threatening to spill. No matter how many times we get hurt, we both can't stand to see each other leave. We walked down the white halls and we took a different route than usual. We walked up to a room that said "water room" my heart instantly starts pounding. The last time I had dealt with water is when they wanted my telethapy to be stronger, they basically waterboarded me the whole time. Out of all the powers I have it is the only one that I struggle with. It seems as if I can't get it to be stronger no matter what they or I do.

We walked into the room and there was a giant pool in the middle of it. There was nothing else except for stairs to climb out of the water, and a white suit hanging on the wall that had straps and buckles going in all types of directions. The water looked very deep the closer we got to it. The only thing I could think about was praying I didn't drown.

They walked me near the wall where the suit was. "Put this on." the doctor said.

I slowly put the suit on over my clothes and strapped it up with all the difficult buckles. I turn around to one of the doctors to signal I'm done. He calls me over to him as he gives me a small metal button and points to the side of his face. I copy his motion and put it on the side of my head as it sticks on. I press the button on the small device and a transparent covering surrounds my face.

"Step inside the pool." The doctor says slowly pushing me closer to the vastly large pool.

I gulped and look at the doctor hoping he wouldn't let me into there.

"Do I have to get in there? Please, I don't want to go, don't make me go in there, please." I know this isn't going to change their minds, but it doesn't hurt to try.

"Get inside. Now." The doctor says without sympathy.

I feel my eyes water as I hold on the rail that leads into the pool. I must of underestimated how deep it is, because as I step off the final step I tried to feel the bottom of it hoping I could stand but there was nothing. I start to panic as I think about the fact that I never learned to float, I'm literally going to drown. I start gasping and reaching to the top as my body slowly sinks. I was hoping the doctors would help, but they continue to watch me sink.

My tears fall freely down my face but I couldn't feel them as the water splashes around me.

"Help! Please help me! I'll do whatever you want just please help!" I beg loudly as the doctors continue to look on with a stoic expression.

This is how I die. I always thought I would've died of old age, or maybe I had a heart attack, or maybe I would even sacrifice myself and died heroically. But instead I'm dying by drowning as a bunch if asshole doctors watch.

I stop moving as I let fate guide me and I fully submerge under water as the water enters my lungs. I scream but more water burns through my throat. I fully sink to the bottom as I feel the darkness surround me. I blackout and wait patiently for whatever is after death. I see a bright light come as I reach after it. I then see a dark figure emerging from the light. It looks like a male figure, but it looked like the figure could be some sort of creature. Is this how God looks?

I scrunch my eyes so I can see more of it. The male/ creature figure reached its hand out and spoke to me.

"Joy."

Those were the only words heard until suddenly everything disappears and I'm back to the surface.

I gasp loudly as I cough up the leftover water in my throat. The doctors hover over me as one of them grabs my face roughly and analyzes me. Theu grab the lottle device thay was on the side of my face before I shove their hands out of my face. I stand up quickly and run towards the door. I pull and bang on it as I hopelessly try to open it. I hear their footsteps slowly coming behind me.

"Please let me out, leave me alone please!" I say as I collapse fully to the ground.

The doctors simply grab me as they lead me out the room. I struggle against them but stopped when one of the doctors pulled out a romote that sent shocks up me collar. I wince painfully and stop all movement while they lead me back.

I thought they were going to take me back to the cage, but we took another route. We walked up to a door with no numbers as they toss me in forcefully.

I don't even fight it as I lay on the hard floor accepting my situation. I try to look around the room, but it's all pitch black. I turn on my back as I sob loudly while tears flood my face continuously. I don't think I can go any longet like this. As much as I try to fight to survive, everyday is harder than the last. I want to try to live for my family, for my friends, even for Logan, but not for myself. I don't believe I can live anymore. I don't want to escape, I don't want to have hope, I don't want anything anymore.

I just want to die.

I look around at the black room and shut my eyes softly. I find comfort in the dark as I let myself succumb to it. I lay silently enjoying the small peace I can have. My crying slowly but surely stops.

I allow myself to think, really think. I think about my Dad and how I hope he's out his coma and living his life fully, and same with my sisters. I hope they are with my dad and are learning how to control the powers the right way. I think about Megan and how much fun we would have at school. We used to hate waking up having to learn 8 hours of random shit, but now thats all I hope I can get back to. I think about the outside world and wonder what was made of it. Did things go back to normal? Was there a way to fix our abilities? Do we now live and accept that most of us have powers? Endless questions about society that I would hope I could find out. But lastly I think of Logan. I think about our love, something that I would beg to have. When I first saw Logan I believed it was a dream, a dream that wasn't attainable. I soon believed that with him, dreams could come true. He taught me a lot of things that I could never forget.

I just hope that if I don't die in here, everyone that I live will be there waiting for me with open arms. Although currently nothing seems possible.

I continue to think in the dark about everything. I laid there for a couple of hours until a brightness shines through. I look to the door wondering if someone had opened it, only to find out I'm not in the room anymore. I look at the shining, bright light again as the same figure from earlier comes into sight.

The brightness of the light slips away as I can fully see the figure this time. I look up and see who the creature is. It's Logan.-------

# Not Any Longer

I stare at Logan in actual disbelief. First Megan and now Logan? I know I was becoming crazy by being here, but I didn't think I would be this crazy.

He makes small paced steps towards me as if he's afraid I'll dissapear from him. He is in his monster form, but I don't feel afraid as he comes closer to me.

"Joy, I've finally found you." He says- more like thinks, but I can hear his voice in my head. His voice is rough and sounds like a growl as he spits his words.

"Logan- I- I don't know what to say." I say still staring in disbelief.

"I'm just happy to see you after all this time. You don't know how badly I've been needing to see you." He says crouching down to me on the floor.

So he didn't find another super powered chick to date?

Fine by me.

"All I've wanted all this time was you." He says, chuckling while gliding his sharp finger across my face. Even though his fingers aren't soft I still find comfort in his touch, as his rough fingers lower themselves onto my neck as he slowly lets his arm drop.

So I must be imagining, because there is no way I can feel him right? There is no possible way Logan is here. Although I feel as if I'm losing my mind I think I'm going to accept this feeling. I forgot what it felt like to come in contact with another human who isn't going to strike me down.

"I'm not actually here, here, but I am real and I can feel you just as much you can feel me. I can't belive I'm here touching you just as you can't believe that I'm here."

I scrunch my eyebrows confused. If he was actually here, the guards would have already come and probably tried to kill us, so how is he here? Before I could ask Logan turns into his human form. Unlike all the other times he turns back, he's fully clothed. He grabs my hands and lifts me off my back as I sit on my butt. He sits in front of me still holding my hands. I stare at his soft features and tears start forming as it's felt like forever since I've seen him.

I let go of his hands and pull him close. I sort of sit on his lap and he holds me just as tight as I hold him. I let out a small sob as I lay my head closer into his neck.

I forgot it all. I forgot about the comfort, the touch, and the feelings I felt for him. I couldn't belive that I let this place make me forget what it felt like to love. I look up from his neck as he's already looking down at me with unshed tears.

"Joy before our time is over I need to tell you something important." He says sniffling.

I nod in understanding and get off his lap but still sit closely next to him.

"Today you are going to escape." I look at him even more confused.

Just when I thought he is actually real, here he goes telling me I'm about to leave this place. Sure.

He pinches the bridge of his nose as he continues. "Look I know you don't believe me, but it's true I'm going to tell you how to do it."

"Logan, I know you have a big heart and you believe, that is one of the many things I love about you. But this, me escaping, don't give me false hope about it. I don't need another day of me praying to someone that I will make it out. I'm not escaping, Logan. I will most likely die here." I say touching his hand. He holds my hand tighter giving me a sense of strength.

"You are making it out Joy, you are making it out of here alive, today. I have an understanding that you have been talking to Megan?"

Wait. How did he know about me and Megan? From what I know me and her only talked once and she disappeared infront of me.

"Yes I talked to Megan, the same way I'm talking to you, but she wasn't real, the same say you aren't real."

"I've already explained I'm real. But forget that, she told me that you have no idea that you've talked to her in the past, but I'm hoping you remember the last time you talked to her."

I scrunch my eyes trying to remember. "I do recall talking to her, but I thought it was a dream. For starters she told me to remember.

Remember what exactly, I'm not sure. Then she told me that you-" I look at Logan for a second taking him in. He looks down at me expecting me to continue.

"She told me you escaped. I wanted to believe it, because you could've made it out and been having a good life, but I also didn't want to believe her." He looks at me confused as to what I mean.

"I didn't want to believe her, because if I did then I would have to deal with the fact that all this time you were out you didn't find me. Maybe you didn't try or maybe you did and gave up and soon completely forgot about me. I know its selfish of me, but if I got out I would've looked for you, so I would only hope you would do the same. But in the end I can't be mad if you didn't want to find me, I would just be a burden that you would hold onto." I finish while tucking legs to my chest.

He just stares at me with wide eyes. I hear him sigh as he scratches his head. "Joy, I know it's been a long time since we've last seen each other, hell it's been a long time since everything, but believe one thing. I never forgot about you. You were the one thing that kept me strong while being tortured, starved, and beaten. The idea that I could see you again made me forget about the pain I was enduring.

You are the reason I fought so hard. You are the reason I am here right now. All because of you Joy. I know it took me quite some time, and I'm so sorry for that but I found you right now and I'm not letting you go this time." He ends up pulling my hands from underneath my knees and holds them to his chest. I blink not expecting him to admit that.

I know I has my doubts about him loving me, but hearing him say it out loud brought the upmost comfort in me. "Thank you Logan, I needed to hear that." I reply softly.

"Of course, anytime Joy. But we need to talk about you leaving. Megan has been speaking to me the same way I'm speaking to you. Telepathically. We have been trying to reach you for some time now, but you seemed harder to connect to then others."

I flinch at that sentence as that's exactly what the whitecoats claimed I have been struggling with. That's one of the many reasons they put me through countless 'exercises'. And it's the exact reason Logan and Megan couldn't find me. All because I was too weak.

"Joy you are not weak. Just because we had a hard time finding you doesn't make you weak, it means we needed to be stronger to find you. Besides none of that matters now. We've finally found you and you're coming with us."

"Did Megan escaped?" I question.

"No not yet, she stayed in captivity to strengthen her powers to get to you. She told me how to speak with you so that I can give you hope. She said the last couple of times that you spoke to her, you seemed like you wanted to quit. I won't let that happen."

I nod my head slowly.

"How come I don't remember speaking to her?"

It would be really nice to know what me and Megan spoke about. I could've left this place long ago if that was the case.

"I'm assuming they tortured you too much. They seem to want your telepathic powers to grow, so they probably pushed you too far to the point where it was more damaging, then helpful." He says rubbing my fingers in small circles.

"That makes sense they did put me in electro-therapy a little too much." I chuckle trying to feel better.

Logan just stares at me not finding my comment funny. I clear my throat feeling slightly awkward.

"So how am I leaving?" I ask trying to move past the awkwardness

"You need to talk to Megan. She will give you all the information you need and then you will escape."

"Why are you talking to me then?" Not that I'm not happy to see Logan, but I'm just curious why Megan couldn't be here.

"I already said Megan and I believe I will give you the hope that you need and she believes that me being here will let you connect more telepathically which should lead you to remember the conversation more. Its easier to telepathically connect with someone when you feel a stronger connection or emotion to them."

Logan speaks as if he's studied this for some kind of test. How much did he really know about this or powers in general? Does the world now offer supernatural classes to teach people about powers? Did the world really adapt to people like us? Seems unlikely as people fear things they don't know, but because there is so many of us maybe they just had to accustom to powers.

"Logan how do you know this?"

"Joy the world that we once knew is well... gone."

Well there goes my answer

"People don't necessarily live the same way we used to. We kind of live in groups. People fight to stay on top. We fight for food, basic needs and well, its overall a whole dystopia. We have to survive out here. Nobody knows why the government just gave up or why people in general gave up, but it's nothing like how it was before." He says looking uneasy.

So what I'm hearing is life doesn't really get that much better. I mean I don't care how bad it is outside of here it has to be better then getting tortured every waking hour, but still it's a disappointment to hear that.

"What about you Logan how do you survive out there?"

He looks at me with some kind of guilt then looks away.

"That's not important what's important is you leaving now. Your sisters and mine are very much alive and are in the same facility as each other. Your dad is also alive but is still in a coma. We have tried everything to reach him but he doesn't seem like he is making it out of the coma."

I really had hoped my father was out of his coma, but from what I'm hearing about the outside world, it seems like he is better in a peaceful, soundless sleep.

"He's ok though right? He's not like dying or anything in his coma, he's just lying asleep peacefully?"

"We can't tell he just lies there with no movement, no function, no anything really. But from the looks of it he seems perfectly fine."

I let out a breath I didn't know I was holding, that's all I needed to hear.

"And my sisters, have you guys contacted them anyway? Is your sister fine?"

"Well fine wouldn't be the word I use. But they are alive. They do get tortured the same way we do so it's best if we find them quickly. We have talked plenty today. I will talk more when I see you tonight, I need you to talk to Megan now." He says standing from the ground lifting me up as well.

I stand face to chest with him as I look up at him with watery eyes. He touches under my cheek where the eye that is purple is at, as if he just realized my eye is a new color. I shut my eyes turning away from him letting his hand drop to his side.

"Logan I don't think I can do this. I want to belive that I could leave and meet up with my family like a perfect, little fairytale, but I don't think I can. What if I don't make it our, what if I think I made it out and it was all just a dream, what if talking to you right now is just a dream? How am I supposed to believe I can make it out if I can't even believe in myself?" I'm still turnt away from him as he grabs my shoulder softly.

"We didn't make it this far so you to fail. You didn't live this far for you to tell yourself that you don't believe. Your sisters, your dad, Megan, and me, Joy, we are waiting for you and we know that you will do it. Don't ever think for a second that you are less than what you are. Once you escape you will see us. We will be together again and don't think that we have ever doubted you. If you believing in yourself isn't enough, just know that all of us believe in you." He finishes as he turns me around fully and grabs my waist.

"And most of all I believe in you the most." He kisses my forehead tenderly as I relish in his touch. He holds me tightly to him while he puts his head in top of mine.

"Close your eyes for me." He speaks softly as I comply.

"Take a deep breath in and let it slowly slip out of your body. All you need to do is think about Megan and think about talking to her. Every little detail you can think of her, let it come to you and imagine she's right infront of you. Feel the emotion of how you would feel if you finally saw her and let her become to life. I know you can do this Joy. I never gave up on you Joy so dont give up on me, on anyone you have ever loved. I believe in you." He says as he slowly slips away.

I feel the grip on my body strengthen even as he slips away from me I feel worried because I think I'm not going to see him again, but I hear him repeating over and over how much he believes in me. I let go and start imagining Megan infront of me.

I think of all the memories we had. All the laughter and fun, I think about the small mole on her face and her curly hair bouncing in the wind. I imagine I'm with her right now, experiencing these moments all over again until I open my eyes and suddenly she's right here with me.

A small smile graces her lips as she runs up to me and squishes me tightly.

"I knew you could do it." She pushes me away from her while keeping her arms on my shoulders.

"I think it's about time we leave, what do you think?"-----

www.ingramcontent.com/pod-product-compliance
Lightning Source LLC
Chambersburg PA
CBHW071450080526
44587CB00014B/2053